The Preacher of Death

Der Todesprediger

by

Gustav Landauer

1893

Translated by David Grunwald

Le contr'etat

Introduction

This book, written by one of the greatest modern Anarchists, has never been published in the English language. It was written by the world's foremost thinker on contemporary anarchism. Gustav Landauer was as misunderstood as the philosophy which he died defining. He came of age at a confluence of ideas taking place at the turn of the 20th century. Innovation and a promise of a better tomorrow filled the thinking of the pre-World War One generation. How bitter would be their disappointment at the abject destruction wrought in the muddy, corpse strewn fields of World War One Europe.

Some argue that hope for mankind died in 1914 and has never been resurrected. Landauer built a life defining a new way of thinking about living, community and the purpose of humanity. His ideas, considered dangerous by the right-wing Freikorps, led to his brutal murder in prison May 2, 1919 shortly after the fall of the short-lived Munich Socialist Republic where he served as Minister of Culture and Education.

This is Gustav Landauer's first book which he called "my book" or "my Story". It is the story of a widower who finds his way is perhaps an old story. It is a strange story, with little action and a lot of philosophy. Landauer republished it in 1903 and regretted that be had not had the time to perform any necessary revisions. Charles Maurer in his fascinating book "Call to Revolution: the mystical anarchism of Gustave Landauer" writes that *Der Todesprediger* "has nearly all the elements that constitute Landauer's vision of a better life for mankind. If he failed to articulate here the reality he understood, he made up for it by spending the rest of his life at the task.

His belief in the validity of that reality never wavered.

Gustav Landauer was born in 1870, the second child in a working-class family in Karlsruhe in South-West Germany. The book "The Preacher of Death" (*Der Todespradiger*) appeared in 1893. Along with the 1903 book "Skepticism and Mysticism" (*Skeptik und Mystik*), it contains a set of ideas that remained with Landauer until his brutal murder at the hands of the German far right Freikorps on May 2, 1919. In a prison courtyard an officer struck him across the face, the signal for a savage massacre. Set upon by the troops, Landauer was beaten with truncheons and rifle butts, kicked, stomped and trampled upon. 'Kill me, then!'

he exclaimed, 'to think that you are human beings!" These were his last words. At that he was shot to death. The perpetrators included Kapp, Lüttwitz, and Seargent Digele. All were acquitted for following orders.

The Preacher of Death was one of Landauer's first books and it captures the nascent anarcho-socialist ideas that he would develop into an expression of Nietzsche's early liberation philosophy. Before releasing Skepticism and Mysticism twenty years later, Landauer wrote a short statement on the re-release of The Preacher of Death:

"Now that I have reread these stormy confessions taken from an excruciating, happy, capable and, thank God, brave youth, I almost wonder how ironic the external experiences of this Starkblom." He called the book "a harbinger of that great revolution that was mistakenly forgotten to be made at the end of the nineteenth century." He added that "the tiredness and interesting pallor that looks so graceful on some of our youth today is probably also due to the great deeds that their fathers failed to do. So, it is something like inhuman socialism, and anarchism turned away from the world, that can be found in this book: A revolution that has turned inward." In hoping that the book would find its generation, Landauer was swimming in the mighty currents of fin de siècle Europe with its feverish restlessness, blunted discouragement, fears of imminent perdition and extinction along with the idea of an inward rebellion against the forces of modernism that would claim so many lives in the bloody 20th century.

Erich Hobsbawm was correct when he wrote that "the very volunteerism and primitiveness of theory that characterized many anarchists and libertarians before WWI was their very asset."

The fundamental ideas of Landauer are presented in what Friedrich Engels called a *"Tendenzroman"* or "political novel." His ideas of community, history, revolution and utopia are woven into the transfigurative story of the main character, Karl Starkblom.

James Horrox writes: Landauer's middle-class origins, his uncompromising pacifism and disdain for the sterile dogmatism and reductive rationalist arguments of many of the dominant theories of his day meant that he spent most of his life ostracized by the bulk of the mainstream European workers' movement. Nevertheless, the philosophy he put forward points to a level of insight into human psychology and the nature of social relationships uncommon among anarchists of his time and many, particularly the more intellectual factions within the European Left, recognized that the populist Romantic strain underpinning his ideas actually brought his unique brand of anarchism closer to accounting for the complexity of the human being than theories which reduce the manifold intricacies of human existence to the simplistic rigidity of two battling classes.

Landauer believed that above all the *Geist* in the individual was key to creating a better world. He used Marx's belief that technology creates society and then rejected Marxism as a "steam engine" and blamed it for forgetting the spiritual side of the workers it purported to serve while in effect creating a society filled with dogma, misery and workers barracks.

Fellowship and community as handed down from Kropotkin and Proudhon were part of Landauer's ideology that the state itself was artificial and unable to advance mankind. For Landauer, the dynamic forward was not leadership from above, but from below.

His thorough research into the French Revolution showed that the French "sections" organized from some 60 Parisian districts created real communities from the bottom up. In Landauer's later 1909 translation of Proudhon's "The French Revolution: Districts and Sections in Paris 1789" he wrote:

Foubert also pointed out: "In this way the revolutionary movement was directed just as much against centralism as against despotism." At the beginning of the revolution, the French people seemed to have understood that the immense transformation which was their task could not be accomplished either by constitutional means or by a central authority: it had to be the work of local forces who, in order to act, had to have great freedom. Perhaps it was also thought that the conquest of freedom had to begin in every village and every town."

As editor of *Der Sozialist* newspaper, Landauer shared translations of thinkers and philosophers, Proudhon in particular. In an article appearing on 1910 he put forth the following limitation of Marxism taken from Proudhon: "What is valid in economic matters for the simple private individual becomes wrong the moment you scale it to the entire society."

The Hegelian dynamic of history was to be replaced by the Landaurean concept of transformations striving for *Utopia*, always alive even in revolutionary times, which fails and results in "*Wahn*", or revolution on the way to a new utopia. Thus, history is always in the process of becoming, a concept he called

"*Werden*". In his understanding, one "topia" is replaced by another with a remnant of the dying still carried in it.

Others commented on the paradox between the old way and the new way that emerged and found its way into protests against the pathos of a dying century. Gustav Landauer was one of those writers for whom the new century exposed the loss of structure and purpose, order and defined status.

In its place would be a new relationship with the state and a restoration of the community commonly associated with medieval or trifunctional societies that had been replaced by anonymous, centralized states thereby destroying the *Geist*, or spirit of the individual. He railed against the conception of law, secularization, absolutism, atomized masses and egotistical individualism.

It was Landauer that wrote famously: The State is a condition, a certain relationship between human beings, a mode of behavior; we destroy it by contracting other relationships, by behaving differently toward one another... We are the State and we shall continue to be the State until we have created the institutions that form a real community."

Charles Maurer writes that Landauer was "the first thinker who combined a thinking of community with the breakdown of certainty. As a result, he demonstrated the extreme consequences of a skeptical definition of politics and an anarchic conception of time. This can be used, Maurer argued, to develop a more philosophical thinking of community as a bond between human beings, beyond dogmatic assumptions and technical accounts of politics."

The inscription on Landauer's tombstone taken from his famous work *"Anruf zum Sozialismus"* reads *"Es gibt jetzt noch Opfer anderer Art zu bringen, nicht heroische, sondern stille, unscheinbare Opfer, nun für das rechte Leben ein Beispiel geben"*. It is the time for different sacrifices, not heroic, but tranquil and unseen sacrifices to give an example of a better life.

To that end, the Preacher of Death is perhaps the earliest manifestation of the blend of vitalistic Nietzschean individuality and socialist communism. In developing the idea of "inner revolution", Landauer boldly posited that "revolution is not what the revolutionaries think it to be."

Landauer places *"Geist"* or spirit in a central role as a force that 'withdraws into the individual genius who live without a "Volk" or people: lonely thinkers, poets and artists, who without security, as if uprooted, stand almost in the air.' If socialism is ever to come, he believed it would need to come from the *Geist* — out of the depth of our inner need and our inner wealth.

The words contained in Landauer's *Preacher of Death* have never been published in the English language. The ideas contain almost all the elements of Landauer's vision of a better life for humankind. His belief in the validity of these ideas never wavered.

Ruth Link Salinger in her book "Gustav Landauer Philosopher of Utopia" writes the two most interesting and incomplete attempts at [humanistic] renewal were Landauer's book Skepticism and Mysticism published in 1903 and his participation in the Munich Revolution in 1918-1919. It was a decade earlier that the 20-year old Landauer wrote The Preacher of Death which was autobiographical and paved the way to the 1903 work. The two works should be taken together to give a full picture of Germany's most famously undiscovered anarchist.

Perhaps Gustav Landauer has finally found what he desired over a century ago — an audience for his ideas and a willingness to think inwardly and make a better society by placing community over centralism. Another writer, La Boétie, asked where the tremendous power of the tyrant came from. He responded that it was the habit of complacency. And the habit of man was more powerful than nature itself.

The Discourse on Voluntary Servitude (*Discours de la servitude volontaire ou le Contr'un*), a work attributed to Étienne de La Boétie by Montaigne, was published clandestinely in 1577. The main thrust was that *le Contr'un* meant to be in servitude under a single power. Boetié believed this proclivity of ours to server under a dictatorial power amounted to an "internal flaw" in humankind.

Gustav Landauer saw it differently. In the end it was mankind's ability to put community over state that led to a better society: *Le contr' etat.*

Der Todesprediger - The Preacher of Death
(1893)
by Gustav Landauer

The story I wish to tell happened during a happy time. The planets circled around the sun without a wherefore or why and the sun shone without question, its rays shining without a care. The self-philosophizing epoch had yet begun and the pain of the words and the great wailing of the cosmos that preceded its dissolution into pure nothing had yet to occur. Yet the general condition of earthly bodies came to differ; for the sharp observer in menacing symptoms, a danger revealed itself. The whole earth was gradually covered in a greenish mold that mirrored in a sort of bad copy, the world of beasts. Everyone from largest to smallest went their own way, looked out for themselves and cared not in the least for another. Happiness in this world consisted of thoughtless independence. Miserable creatures emerged on the face of this moldy earth who had nothing but each other to lean on and fight against. Gradually, a species, bereft of individuals and persons grew. A tiny germ of consciousness or the capability for it, lay in every nook and cranny of the earth. A kind of poison gained dominion over the beings which brought them to a state of self-destruction which arose from self-confidence, and transformed into self-contempt and pain. This role had been the fate of human beings for some time. It is left to history to tell of this strange species of animal and how it approached its ambitions. I could already foresee, with a quick look to the whole of history, a point when self-loathing and individual pain exceeded a level and transformed itself into worldwide sorrow.

Although interrupted at times, the long developing and slow progression and selfish grasping has lasted for several centuries. Christianity, the Reformation and Rationalism were attempts at healing but they ultimately failed. Then came a brief period of resignation and desperate pain. Unenlightened men were the leading spirits and, in the background, emerged subtle figures existing in melancholy calmness exhibiting aristocratic, priestly manners without backbone or will.

Then came an eternally memorable attempt by cold blooded reason to review all past development of human history and the current goings-on and wash the hands of the past and start the life of mankind from scratch after careful examination.

I wish to tell the story of these past years, when men lived together in exhaustion and abject misery.

Part One

Max Emanuel Karl Wilhelm was the second son of the shoemaker Adam Starkblom and his wife Elisabeth; People called him Karl. He had two sisters, Elise und Kathrine, and five brothers: Adam, Justus, Lebrecht, Friedrich and Johannes. The father had been able to support the family, but later, due to his phlegmatic and contemplative temperament gradually he lost sobriety and gave in to drink. He died of a heart attack at 64 years of age. The father's stages of life were shared by his children. Adam followed his inclinations and apprenticed at a large trading company in Hamburg, and eventually became a large plantation owner in Haiti. Karl became a student. Elise attended a school for women and married a wealthy locksmith at nineteen years old. Justus had apprenticed to his father and now owned a small shoe factory in Pirmasens. Lebrecht became a distiller. Johannes was completed adrift and finally was called to Haiti by the oldest brother. There he was fired from his position truck driver and disappeared. Katherine, the youngest, had gone into the opera theater, became a mistress of a wealthy officer and eventually a prostitute. The mother was laid up in bed after childbirth; it was no wonder that the child left behind in the house of a drunkard didn't get the best upbringing.

Karl had held a special position in his parent's house. He participated reluctantly in the noisy games of his brothers and sisters, preferring to go his own way. He was a loner and a dreamer who could not open up. By his 9th year he had voraciously read many books in his father's house often rereading things that interested him. He came to know large parts of novels by heart. By 15, he had stopped reading almost entirely in this way and developed a plan: he read classics, literary history, religious works and philosophy. What he did not understand, he quietly put aside and he memorized those things he read frequently. He enjoyed spending time with his sister Elise and her girlfriends and soon got a reputation as asocial and was mocked as a person who spent most of his time with girls. At the table when the parents and siblings were present, he was quiet and self-conscious. But if a topic interested him. he could become quite voluble in expressing himself; For this reason, he was labelled as an old-fashioned and precocious child. At school he was considered among the top of his class because he understood quickly and had a good memory although he did little work. His teachers disliked him, some even despised him. He rarely responded to questions although he knew the answers. Sometimes he stood there calm and pale, dreaming without opening his mouth. At other times he became passionate with what he knew or meant; he had even dared to correct his teachers a few times.

Before he was sixteen years old, he was determined to study philosophy and solve the puzzles of the world. Before finishing school, he gave up on it. He saw how his father had ended and it made sense to him to take a practical job. He replied calmly to all the questions about what he would study: Jurisprudence, and he stayed with it. So, he decided not to read any more philosophy books and took to school work in an effort to gain an understanding of daily life and interests. At eighteen, he graduated high school and moved on to the university. He found friendship in his last years of school when his inclination toward philosophy emerged.   Earlier he had no need to deal with such things. Deep and original opinions pressed him in conversations with friends. There were so many young people striving at the same time many did not see eye to eye. In the beginning there was a philosophical society with plenty of things to do. They organized themselves into an association and adopted their own statutes. Later Karl abandoned the society and travelled with three friends with one intimate friend in whom he confided his boldest thoughts and plans. At first, he wrote his ideas down in a diary and worked a few of them into longer pieces. He gave that up too when he saw that his opinions changed too quickly and he still had no firm position; from then on, he pursued them with coolness and a certain curiosity of his own. This time he didn't pay too much attention to his new thoughts because he knew how quickly the old ones had always evaporated. After his decision to become a lawyer, he retired from the few remaining friends he had; He didn't want to be tempted to go too deeply into himself and the wisdom of the world in order to turn his attention to the practical work of a civil profession. Since it doesn't really work to do two things. What he thought of as heroic was viewed contemptuously by all others.

He became a hard-working student, working with the colleagues had gotten to know. He deliberately refrained from social amusements. It was here in the practical discussions with friends at the beer table that he began to come into his own. He became something more than average. He thought clearer, judged everything from a higher perspective and summed up distant things in an elegant way. He became absorbed in problems, especially theoretical problems and became more concerned with the question of details. As he wrestled with these details it came to him more than once: Wait! I'm still myself! Nothing is finished! I am not completely wise to the world and haven't ignored the study of law; But underneath, my search continued. My old philosophies would rise up and disappear amongst new thoughts that seemed to roll over me. From whence they came, I knew not. But wait! The preacher in the desert is not yet dead! And when he comes again, he will be right on time! Karl would expel such thoughts again, then lean on his thick books and stare deep into the night.

In the last few years of his studies, when the others were just starting out, he closed his books and took a break. He reached a point where he felt he had learned enough for the exams. A new person awoke in him. He became sociable, cheerful and suddenly learned to make small talk. He learned to dance, fell in love with a pretty girl and got engaged secretly. However, soon this cosmopolitan life ended. Once again, he became quiet and detached. He didn't feel comfortable in society, took to himself and forgot the gossip and small talk. When the exams came, he passed them with flying colors.

Afterwards, he served a year with his infantry division in his hometown. He prohibited himself mental activity; he was just a soldier, inside he was sullen and removed, while on the outside, strict and disciplined. He returned to practicing law, gained an internship and after passing the second level of exams, climbed the ladder of promotion. Even as a student he had made the decision to stay in the civil service and become a judge. After a long period of dating, he married his sweetheart and started a household. He was close to a judgeship but still needed more earnings. He borrowed from his brother Adam who was doing well in his ventures in Haiti.

The marriage seemed to be an extremely happy one; Karl was calm and serious and this made wife calm and cheerful; she had a tremendous respect for her husband's spirit and was able to understand and engage in his career with him. His work consumed him. From that point on he cared less for other things. He had little interest in art or theater and found little time for politics. He came to say over and over, "Hold on! I've become an old man! But I was once so young!" Misfortune gripped him and didn't let up: their first child, a girl, died after struggling for two days, the second child, another girl, died of pneumonia after three months and a third pregnancy, this time a boy, ended with the death of the mother and child.

After five years of marriage, Karl Starkblom was once alone in the world. While he remained calm on the outside, day and night he was plagued by questions that left him no peace. "What should I do now?" "What is there to live for?" "Why now have you taken my one reason for living?" "Oh, what a time for this!"

As if fate wanted to leave him no doubt, another death occurred several months later: his brother Adam in Haiti suddenly dies of a fever and left him a great fortune bequeathed to Karl in his will. He was just 42 years old. He had served as a district judge for almost 3 years. His inner voice told him to stop and let up a bit. He headed for a rest to a little town in the Black Forest. A little while later he retired after careful deliberation.

His colleagues made snide remarks about his decision to retire early. Up until now everyone considered him ambitious in his pursuits in pursuing making as much money as possible and perhaps being a closet hedonist; nevertheless, the large inheritance suited him well. Now he could pursue things without the burdens imposed by work. Now the high browed gentleman showed his true colors. An aristocrat who could not deny his common origins. What blank faces people would have made had he entrusted to them his real reasons: abandoning his chosen profession and now fully intending to live out his life in the spirit and aspirations of his early youth. His ambition was none other than living out his youth. Buts was this even possible? Did he have it in him? What was left of his youthful ideals? What could he bring to humanity?

He looked into his own soul and discovered that beneath the calm exterior lay sadness and pain at the core. It was then and there that he noticed that misery and pain pervaded all of humanity throughout the whole world. As he had grown from an innocent child to a man, he had quickly forgotten the blossoming of a sense of the world; external circumstances were to blame. Now as a mature man who had tasted all the pain and delights that a man can have; he then experienced the philosophical despair and social misery stormed with full force and all at once. It seemed in that moment that he had slept more than twenty years, dreamt of useless things. Now he began to look around and think seriously about the human spirit and the purpose of the world. Thoughts swam in his head, such moods as he had not experienced in a long while and yet it was as if he had thought it all before even a thousand years ago.

It occurred to him that he should go back to his old diaries and notes. As he read them, he no longer understood many things and misunderstood a good many other things. Some things gave him a great many different meanings at the time; but some things stayed the same and were uttered in almost the same way. These emerged as new truths. He was terrified of himself, the student and the judge, how could it have happened? Would he be able to find himself again? And a quiet joy came over him. He was young again.

"I want to dedicate my services to mankind; I want to speak new words no one has ever uttered."   He had written these very words at sixteen years of age and now he wanted the same again.   He felt the strength in him and was equal to the task — a match for anyone.

Initially he intended to stay in the sunny little town he currently resided in. The solitude would do him well. He needed time to reflect. In nature he could rejuvenate himself in the lush green forest; his poetic imagination, long slumbering, was now waking from a sleep as he listened to the song of the birds and soaked up sunlight.

One morning in the cool spring weather he went along the river to the town in the valley. He especially liked this way. As the trail wound around the mountains, he saw hills to the side and mountains in front of him with ever new shapes and colors. On the right was the river. Lush meadows lay beyond and further away the mountains were covered with dark pine forests. Looking around, he saw the city with the high chimneys in the distance; the broken hammer blows quieted as he passed the city. His mind was lively and enterprising and his thoughts spun around in his head. He dreamed more than he thought. It was the first of summer and a heavy thunderstorm had passed through in the early morning. The moving clouds pushed past the sun, briefly darkening the valley. Soon the shadows dispersed and he happily went on his way. After less than a half hour walking, he saw a white shimmering castle-like little house lying on the ledge roughly halfway up the mountain just behind the curve of the river. It greeted him warmly with its white plaster, bright windows, and red tiled roof atop small turrets on the left.

"This would be a great place to live," he thought. He walked on an hour or so then returned to the path that led over the heights. At lunch he told his neighbor, a city planner, about his trip and the little castle he liked so much. He said that the house had been empty for some months since the owner had moved to Vienna. There had been no one interested in it as it was location too remote from the city's manufacturing center. It was a well-known fact that strangers hardly visited the city which was decried as an industrial zone despite its charming surroundings. Starkblom made a quick decision. He visited the lawyer who handled the man's affairs and settled the deal a few days later. He bought the house and over the next few weeks he moved his furniture in and bought some new things. Some of the rooms he left empty for a library. He imagined some exquisite paintings in the future and hired an older woman to cook and run the house.

He moved into the manor on the first of July. Once he got used to it, he was startled at how the little trifles had taken so much of his time over the past few weeks. That all changed. Now he would think great and deep things while the clear waves of the river at the foot of the mountain flowed peacefully toward him.

He procured a large number of books from the city which he read over the next few weeks. As he gave himself to study, he soon realized that it was better to have books than a library and even better to have thoughts than books; experience was even better than the purest thoughts. He had no shortage of thoughts and experiences — he had a whole rich life behind him and delved into memories that had been closed off.

He thought of his father whose life had ended in misery. Certainly, he remembered his earlier better days, how he sat thoughtfully in his shoemaker's chair and offered wisdom with his limited mind about deep problems. Best of all was his gruff, disaffected knowledge that was clouded like the color of the darkish shoe polish he rubbed onto his boots. ... And then mother ... there wasn't so much to remember.

This hard-working woman carried her bundle of hardships with submission and filled her days and nights with murmurs, hums and scolding. She never had much time for her children and certainly not for the lonely Karl. He never knew real love from his mother and even now did not try to reawaken it. The great tender love of his father abided and he always thought of him with sadness. Now that he looked at his own being closely, he unraveled his inherited consciousness and spirit aside from the little things like his walk and posture.

His brothers who lived near him seemed to have vanished and he took no interest in their lives. He often thought of his deceased brother, who had been the impetus of his inner blossoming, with gratitude and less with pain. He had become a capable man with a keen sense for his affairs and energy with a full interest in all things spiritual. In a peculiar way, his thoughts turned to Haiti and the thin outline of a man always in a fog which he tried to see just in front of him. His youngest brother Johannes wanted to celebrate his rebirth. Their relationship as children had been estranged in the way late-born siblings often had superficial things in common; Starkblom sensed what had not occurred to him for a long time. It was a radiance of spirit that occupied his body and that once was lost perhaps forever among people. He remembered the philosophical hours spent with the upperclassmen when some curly haired boy would scurry into the room after wrestling with serious brooding thoughts only to remark that you still had not understood knowledge. It was either childish simplicity or brilliant improvisation. What must have come of this wild Hans? Was he still alive? Starkblom believed he either became a bold man with a clear spirit or had gone to complete ruin; in his hours of dark solitude he could still make out the inky shadows of a man in front of him. It was rare when he brought up the vision of his faithful wife. And then he thought of the three children that had lived such a short time. Then there were times he had hardly felt anything; even now, he thought of his son with a bitter sensation. It was a peculiar feeling, closely related to love: he had been a father! He would have had a smart 5-year old daughter now. A quiet longing for fatherly joy and children's games and raising children often stirred in him.

He would never populate the earth again, this he knew; he could be a person forgoing marriage and children from the outset, transforming the impulse to procreate into a purely spiritual drive. Even such people who do their duty towards their people and humanity are better in some ways that ordinary fathers. And suddenly a horror grew in him. How could he ever have fallen in love like an ordinary person with such foolishness? And marriage? Getting married and witnesses? Looking for sensory pleasure – for years. What requirement was this? How could it be? Was this really who I was? No, no.

O why had he yoked himself to self-interest and convention? Had he made is way without concern for the common lot he would have moved forward in any event! If only he would have ridden it out, he would have remained young! Curse this ugly, ordinary, narrow, depressing interim. Could he ever capture what was missed? He had to catch up with it, to think, live and work. He wanted to be a model, a prophet ... redeemer – was he still youthful enough? Yes, he still believed in himself, he had to; didn't he think of the despair? He looked at himself in the mirror and smiled courageously; he was still young and energetic. His brown eyes still shone brightly, nor did he have the tell-tale, haunted expression around his mouth. The hair on his high somewhat plebian forehead had thinned a bit; but he had no grey hairs in his thick black beard. Certainly, he was still young enough; there was time enough to finish his work. He tried to convince himself of the benefits of his long silence for himself and the world that gave him the gift of thought. What would have become of him if the sudden urge to become a philistine hadn't gripped him as a student? His youthful ideas, taken for untouchable truths might have made him a slave to his first impressions and driven out his own future out of a cowardly consideration for the past for a miserable love of some fleeting success in the moment. He would have exhausted himself early, ahead of time and if he had spoken his first promising words with empty hands and pockets to a world that only wanted to hear the best; but what else could he have offered at that time? It would have been inconceivable luck, if after a long pause, which should now come, he would have gathered himself again in newfound wisdom; but whether one wanted to hear his message — who could say? No, no — better to learn as a youth and speak as a man.

He thought to think carefully about everything he saw without paying particular attention to his own life. All he needed to do was connect thoughts and moods that had racked his soul over the years and the clear world view he knew deep in his heart. His will was decided. He would speak to the people. He had learned that all he needed to do was draw consequences from his life. His motto seemed to be first to live, then to teach. This would be his epitaph, written in advance of the completed first step. It was his long years at Jurisprudence that made complicated things simple and the unordered and chaotic, separated. It made the torn apart appear intertwined, so everything fermented together so unlike cold bottles of pressed abstractions obscuring the hidden desire to foam up any moment? In the end, did the outward appearance of calmness feign peace of mind and a coldness of heart which he did not possess? Did he believe that his will alone remained young and that his mind no longer possessed the drive and force of change possessed in youth? Was his heart then immune from new unanticipated experiences?

At the time such consideration could not be accepted. With cold resolve he had collected his scattered experiences and ideas in order to show the people what he was and what he wanted. Meantime he had lived a lonely spiritual life that was completely independent of the outside world.

He looked back on his previous life as part of his world view and lived so as not to die. But he had moments that came more frequently that he considered grotesque outrages against the idea that he was special, getting older and wanting to rise above his humble beginnings in order to raise up his fellow man.

Was he really different from others? And if so — what was this all for? What did he really want? Did he really have anything to say? Would it not be better to leave people as they are? After all, what concern was it of his? Better perhaps to live with his thoughts in peace and quiet and ponder an eventual death. After all he was not a world-changer made to appear in public.

After all, what exactly was this world? Was there anything to approve and change? He went deeper and deeper into a metaphysical web, his thoughts appearing as the only reality. The world was the product of his senses and his own consciousness. Was it worth trying to change such a transitory appearance, to bring reason into a vain dream, top like trying to improve the shape of a soap bubble? Oh, the world's form may change, but the core remained the same and was unchangeable.

The fresh doubts came to him; wasn't it just the most daring exaggeration to proclaim everything to be riddled with deceit only to justify his thoughts about the world? Wouldn't it be humbler to leave the world alone and doubt the correctness of his own thinking? So, he became more and more dissatisfied and completely robbed himself of the rest of the naivety and zest for live that possessed him previously. All the brooding appeared to him as amateurish, superficial, unprofitable and childish, all due mainly to the need to have an excuse for being out of touch with the world and too lazy to look around.

What else did he want in the world? He decided to find out soon enough.   Did others wish to live unquestioned lives without asking for the purpose put in them by their creator, preferring to vegetate in narrow confines until they died — what did he care about? He felt more and more disgust at the common unconscious way of living among people who didn't have the time or wherewithal to ask what it was all for?

Soon he had days where everything seemed ridiculous, almost crazy. When he walked his mind was half opened to his senses and the world; he kept asking himself: what in the hell is going on here? Everybody running around and working to jealously displace another; and for what purpose? What did you have in mind? Is there any purpose set? Does everyone have their own purpose or is there one single place we are all pointing towards? These things were not being discussed at all. 'Are you kidding yourself?' He muttered as he passed a rock quarry where everyone was busy at work. It all seemed to comedic to me! Who was being fooled? And so, he continued to ponder. Naturally, everyone wanted to show the other person they had a goal they were working towards and everyone else acted as if they believed the other. He passed by a cemetery and thought of another. They had deceived themselves and this was perhaps the main thing. It was death that determined their whole of what they called life. Everyone made as much noise as possible so as not to remember dying, and everyone secretly hoped it was not their turn and they need not die. And because they didn't really believe that, they numbed themselves with petty, superfluous pastimes and called it "living". Was this not madness? If they realized that all of their work would be completely superfluous in the end, if they admitted this to themselves that they would all have to die together, one after another, then they would bring their automatous rattle to a stop and lean their tools and sundry props used in this great comedy against the wall — and what then? Was it not with the greatest indifference whether you died now or in ten, twenty, fifty- or seventy-years' time? Was time really a serious consideration anymore?

No, no. Not in the least. As much as he racked his brain, he found no other purpose for life than death; it all boiled down to it. The fact that you were born only to die was the ridiculous reality in this crazy world. But that was the way it was. Only thing to do was come to terms with it and spread knowledge so that anyone capable of seeing it for what it was could reach the end as quickly as possible.

Or wasn't it? Was it all a tremendous mistake, a dullness of spirit that as long as he tortured his brain, he would not be able to find any other purpose in life? It was this that he had to make certain about. He wasn't the only rational person alive, but he'd not met anyone who shared with such crystal clarity about the naturalness and unchangeability of this shocking insight. I had to ask what the others actually thought of life. "What did you think about life?" He thought he should confront every person he encountered with this question. Whenever he was in town, he observed the people to read their thoughts about their existence, but found nothing of the sort. Their expressions always summed to little ridiculously deceptive things, eating, sleeping, drinking, walking, going to church, out to the theater, cutting wood, gathering coal, heating kettles, patching shoes, sewing shirts, knitting stockings, teaching children, buying vegetables, selling goods, building houses, collecting taxes, drilling soldiers, making laws and giving speeches — always behind a mask, a comedic illusion. Nowhere on any face lay an aspiration or a longing for a something purposeful; Or were they all the smart ones and he the insane? He would have like to have been shown the answer. His thoughts had taken this direction during the first months of his stay in the white house. The contemplative coldness of his mind had disappeared from him after he became involved again with mother earth and her wisdom; a restless, often passionate despair had mastered him. His completely voluntary isolation fostered this. He kept to himself and avoided opportunities where he could have met casual acquaintances or the presence of new people.

After a time, he was overcome with a hunch that it couldn't hurt to get back among people. But he had been unsteadying and needed friends to support him and lead him into other friendly fields of thought. Chance brought him together with an old friend from his youth that he had since lost sight of.

It was on a nice afternoon in the first days of August. He had sunk into the darkness brought by the Canons of Leopardi. The housekeeper brought him a business card. A gentleman waited outside to see whether the doctor could have a word. The card read "Robert Wangaus – Manufacturer". Wanguas — Robert Wangaus, he thought for a moment. He was ashamed he did not realize immediately that name and that he had not thought about him for decades. Have him come in he answered the keeper. He was genuinely happy to see an acquaintance from his youth. Well, so he had become a manufacturer, a professional like himself until recently, he thought. He could have guessed it. He was eager to be what he was. Wangaus, a bold and imaginative as a boy, had been one of his intimate philosophical friends.

A thickset man with a clean-shaven expression entered the room. He placed his silk hat on the chair by the door and set a pair of red-brown gloves atop it. Then he went to Starkblom, who stood and faced him. "So, I was not wrong *Herr Landgerichtsrat*, I recognize in you —."[1]

"But Wangaus," interrupted Starkblom. "I am Karl Starkblom as you are Robert Wangaus. I am very happy about it." Please sit. We want to keep the old you, yes? How are things going with you? You're a manufacturer? Do you live here? Are you married? Please sit down." In the conversation that followed, it became known that Wangaus owned a goldware factory, had been married and lived in the city with his family. He had heard about Starkblom's presence several weeks ago and realized immediately that he was an old acquaintance from the Gymnasium. He

---

[1] *Landgerichtsrat* is translated as "district judge".

had wanted to come earlier, but well what do you know, the delays and business, business, business. "Yes, yes the business", he repeated again and patted a few hairs on the edge of his bald pate. "You, sir, — he apologized for being so formal — I must get used to informality again – well you are certainly well off now. That is said enough, well I don't know what I would do all day long if I didn't have my job."

"Since when has this becomes your life's profession? How?"

"I mean how long has it been since the world became blessed with your jewelry?"

"I am sorry that wasn't expressed exactly. I don't actually make jewelry. I am not sure if you follow the developments of our industry closely. It's taken a huge upswing."

"Well, if you haven't studied the matter, I won't be able to explain it to you shortly. Thing is we only make a certain type of gold that the jewelry factories use to process further. There has been a colossal division of labor; the entire process has become mechanized; I am never bored in general when I find time to delve into theoretical considerations of the modern industry. It is truly wonderful. Just magnificent! How everything weaves together into one whole affair —. Starkblom interrupted him with a delicate mocking smile.

"Oh, you shouldn't laugh at me quoting poetry. I'm a businessman of course with little time, but we all are under the spell of youth so to speak and if I had time, I would still read something of Goethe and Schiller even today." "Do you go to the theater often?" "Theater? Yes, yes, of course. My wife has a box and when she has no time or desire — well, you understand." "Yes, yes, well then Goethe and Schiller will probably come to you more often?" "You mean my wife? Perhaps not. The children attend.

"Classical pieces really are for children, don't you agree?"

"Hm, yes. You know we'd rather not even start arguing about it. Anyway, I'm afraid I am in a very different situation than you. As you wish; say, do you actually have children?" "No." "I never had children."

"Did you?"

"No. I Tried. Three times. The second thought it over for three months whether it wanted to live, but decided otherwise."

"That's hard."

"No. it's not hard. Or did you mean that? What in particular is hard about it? "

"You're not serious. It goes without saying."

"That a man dies sooner or later? Yes, that goes without saying."

"But it really does make a difference whether a small child dies or a man who has completed his life's work. This is simply obvious."

"It's odd that everything is self-evident and clear for you, but it is less clear to me today than ever. Life's work, life's work. How's that? Honestly what is your life's work now?"

"God puts everyone in the place they must take. Nothing is done in vain.   Even if I only use an infinitesimal amount of humanity, after all me with a wife and children. That's my philosophy."

"It's not mine," said Starkblom earnestly as he stood up and paced. "Quite apart from God who it seems to serve   only   two   purposes   today."

"And what would they be?"

"First, he provides an excuse and secondly, makes sensible people nervous.   God puts everything in its place! Ha, ha. I should add you spoke differently in your youth."

"Well, the folly of youth is long behind you. One settles. You're really not serious about all of this? As a manufacturer, I fulfill my duty as we as you perform your duties as a judge — to this very day. "Duty. But duty in the name of who?" "Everyone knows this. Why do you ask about such things?" "Why, not?"

"Again, duty for what purpose?"

"Well, against the others."

"Really? Who calls you to this? How?"

"Why is it you feel the irresistible need to supply humanity with jewelry, but not with a different kind of gold?"

"Well, now that's not so easy to say. These things are complicated. You as a jurist must know these things better than me. After, all you studied the national economy too." "I am still studying it. But still — you see. By the way, you weren't meant to be a jurist. "

"Yes, you are very correct. That you can say against me. But you also know I am no longer a judge."

"Yes, of course. You no longer need to be. You're happier."

"You are mistaken. That wasn't my reasoning. " Now Wangaus smiled. "Well now. Don't kid yourself. If I had gotten an inheritance like yours – well, who wouldn't have acted the way you did?"

"So where is the job and the divine destiny? You were saying? Well, now that doesn't rule out retiring in old age. If you are able of course." "I am not that old yet, on the contrary – my work has just begun." "So?"

"Yes, of course —. So, you've completely given up philosophy?"

"You could say that. Even if I had the time? That wouldn't lead to anything. I don't know. Well, I'd like to try now anyway. "He paused. "Now?"

I mean, I'm going to start working at it like I said. I too wish to make gold."

"What? Are you kidding? That industry is down nowadays. Unfortunately."

"I am speaking figuratively. I won't compete with you. In any event the Wangaus company hasn't anything to worry about."

"Figuratively?"
"I don't understand."

"Yes, I can hardly put in any other way. My job is to think and educate."

Wanguas surveyed the room and saw many books scattered about. "I see, you wish to be a writer? Discuss books, overturn old opinions, create new ones? Well, I wish luck there. At least you have talent. Can make a name for yourself. Or will you write under a pseudonym?"

"Well, not in this case. I'm not really sure if it all boils down to writers. I'm not a particularly fond of paper. Ah, all this is still very vague and seemingly beside the point. It depends on how I approach it. "

"Yes, yes of course there are other ways. The commercial guilds are holding popular lectures everywhere nowadays. If you'd like, I am on the local board and could help you next winter."

"Thank you, but I really don't think that will work for me."

"Well maybe you want to become some big politico? Would you like to apply for a Reichstag seat? You've got a lot of options. For me, I hardly feel the urge to do something like that. But then as I said, it can be done."

"Well, I'm not ready to decide right now but hope to soon."

Wangaus stood up.

"Well, anyway – sorry I couldn't stay longer, I'm off. It was a pleasure to meet you again. Please look me up, you know where to find me."

After a few routine canned pleasantries, he took his top hat and left.

Going down the stairs Wangaus thought to himself: clearly, he is the same old noodle-head. He hasn't changed a bit. Well, hard to believe he was able to become jurist.

Starkblom initially left everything personal aside; the end of the conversation had left him with a psychological perception he had to pursue a bit further. It was strange how two people who have nothing to do with each other can talk together although their natures are so completely different, they must always misunderstand one another. And this is what is called entertaining! He spoke of enlightenment and reality and Wangaus replied with a remark about writers and commercial associations. He indicated his longing to live out his nature and Wangaus thought of ambition and lust for fame. Finally, this good philistine even outdid himself in asking: what for? He replied to all questions with a kind of quietude: For what, for what purpose?   Was he right in the end? Why torture oneself?   But not just to torment yourself? Because he had nothing else to do? Wangaus considered his work to be a serious profession and despised brooding as a useless luxury; yet he himself despised the mindless work done from mere habituation with no reasonable purpose and striving toward any set goal.

He considered deep dives into thinking for the highest purpose.

Which one was the fool? Both?

After the strange meeting with a childhood friend, he had a mind to separate himself even more from people and bury himself in his loneliness.   He just didn't understand such people and it was mutual. He longed to escape this misery and get away from his suicidal broodings. He needed a different approach. People and his own thoughts disgusted him.   — he even though to acquire a large noble intelligent dog. Then he tried a human relationship again.   He fled to Arcadia, to the realm of pure forms — the land of art. The next few days he immersed himself in the finest writing created in German.   He read Goethe's Iphigenie, parts of Faust and Pandora. Coming to Schiller's Bride from Messina after this he closed the book in disgust after a few minutes: even this fare had become to crude and ordinary. He could read no longer. He felt like a wild, grasping animal in a stinking menagerie cage that disallowed for personal agency. Even Leopardi was too subtle for him.

From that point on he was careful not to collide with people and books filled with ideas that might have torn him away from his tranquility which he forced upon himself. He wanted nothing unpleasant, violent or upsetting ... not now anyway. Now he just wanted tranquility. He went to bed early and got up late. Then a lazy breakfast and mornings little meanderings — a little walk through the fir tree forest during which he thought about nothing. Then he read Goethe, Spinoza, Plato and Ranke. He liked the wise old sages best in addition to mystical, romantic and cheerful things: Bretano's *Rosenkranz*, Arnim[2], Eichendorff, Jean Paul, Gottfried Keller.

So, it went for weeks and months. Yet there was something terrible rising up and eating away at any consciousness while living with a superficial well-

---

[2] Carl Joachim Friedrich Ludwig von Arnim (26 January 1781 – 21 January 1831), better known as Achim von Arnim, was a German poet, novelist, and together with Clemens Brentano and Joseph von Eichendorff, a leading figure of German Romanticism. The early German romantics strove to create a new synthesis of art, philosophy, and science, by viewing the Middle Ages as a simpler period of integrated culture.

being.   There wasn't much else to report about him for the time being.

Part Two

People like Karl Starkblom seldom rocked violently from one impulse to another. They often robbed one despair for another. Sooner or later, they moved with inevitable certainty out from human society and into loneliness.   At the time there was a small group in Europe who knew nothing about each other nor did they want anything from each other. They formed no association or party because their faith was too weak for anything existing in the present.

They placed much too much hope in the future.

Every now and then one of them committed suicide. Others looked around and honored the unknown dead and asked themselves what they were actually waiting to die for.

But these few apparitions, who were innocently crazy or mad — the world by and large ignored; for their sake they carried on their duties and modest entertainments calmly and without worry.   But coming from the opposite side, a new teaching had penetrated or emerged from the masses, that one did not know that forward politicians suspected a great revolution. Some philosophical historians wanted to see signs of powerful religious movements. International social democracy had become a world power which required the greatest statesmen to the smallest pastor to come to a reckoning.

The growth of socialism, was most powerfully promoted by the misery of the European bourgeoisie after the French Revolution. The hard, clear conscious of the powerful and the wealthy was gone forever. So many new freedoms and rights were recognized by the population as eternal and inviolable human rights that the miserable society inherited from the conflict between traditional conditions and the fruits that broke its way no longer existed as did inherited freedoms and relations. They were tormented by the evil conscious of having nourished themselves on the blood of the poor and building palaces on the bodies of the common man. There they stood with trembling hands and cross-eyed looks scratching together their little trinkets, and sticking their heads in the sand while covering themselves in phrases for they had no stomach for brutality and no thought for renunciation. In no time flat, what was taught the poor formed such a pitiful contrast with reality; yet they still held belief in teachings and in their lives and tried to be as good as they could. For they never had any doubts about what made the wealthy so strange or they're about their morals. This chaotic anarchy was in fact a fertile bed of manure from which wonderful, outrageous manifestations could spring. That was a time when every possibility grew fresh after long careful preparation and were touted as new redeeming truths and new beliefs were stashed away faster than an outmoded fashion; it was the late times when everything new and unborn was greedily consumed. At that time the extremes touched and the strong and weak found themselves bound together in disgust and resignation. The Russian aristocrat and philosopher alike praised the power of physical labor and renounced their social position to become a farmer and cobbler; at the same time the German shoemaker's son, as lord of the white castle, had disdained plain work. Yet, these two lonely preachers, who shared in disgust, actually belonged together.

These tired abandoned people crept away from the middle-class table; while in social democracy, an organized mass of hungry emerged. Working people stormed the palaces of the spirit. These hordes of purposeful fighters had never been seen before. Their heads contained a strange mixture of imagination and sobriety, passion and restraint, faith and skepticism, and action with deliberation. They recognized the danger of beautiful words and usually guarded against them fearfully. Liberté, égalité, fraternité – what had become of this intoxicating battle cry of the revolution? Freedom?

Never had a more beautiful word been misused. Of course, they were completely free to work under the conditions imposed by capitalism or starve to death. No coercion was exerted, no one compromised their personal freedom. As for equality — well they had become the same proletarian mass. Fraternity and brotherhood had to be added by themselves. It had not been thought of anymore and they wanted to rise up in the name of social democracy. Workers of all lands, unite! This call spread throughout the world, shook the oppressed and united them together for the same purpose; to liberate mankind of anarchic commodity production and distribution, for the communal production and distribution of needs and for the destruction of blind selfishness; for the destruction of national contradictions; to create a real humanity and brotherhood.

Karl Starkblom had seen with a youthful enthusiasm a goal rise up. As he prepared himself for his work among the people, he studied socialist writings, paying particular attention to Karl Marx. A new man, who had slumbered for a long time, now arose in him. It was the impetuous inquirer who sought satisfaction for himself and in doing so wanted to satisfy a timeless longing: What for? Why is it so? Why is it not otherwise? What should be? In this way socialism wanted to make the poor workers human — those who themselves could not fathom the world — but for him socialism could not offer him the final worldview at this time.   So, he had withdrawn from brooding and despair before the crazy search for a new world. He returned to an old dead world view in order to perform a hard reset for the time being.   After so many internal leavenings, another would have stayed put. Young Karl had surrounded himself inside a civil service career and came close to burying himself under the protective blanket offered by a desolate, petrified culture. There was something unspeakable in the man who kept rising against the quietude and numbing confines of a shoemaker's son; something rousing, ambitious and forthcoming; it was the same force that pulled his dead brother Adam to Haiti and Johannes out into the wider world.   His mind worked ahead of his will; hence his detachment and slow awareness, arbitrary stops and the solitary thought.

He was a sturdy man with some years behind him and yet more time ahead; it lay at the core of his essence.

Gradually the tranquil anxiety of his life and the seclusion of this dream began to bore him. His soul slowly migrated to life going on outside and cautiously he groped for places in order to engage with the wider world yet still maintain his inner peace. He sensed there still could be joy in him and perhaps a belief. He was tired of the clever bondage that represented his life and prepared for happy ignorance and rapture.

It was on a beautiful clear winter day when there was something like freshness and courage and a tender zest for life with him. Who knows where he got the idea to find an old pair of skates and set off for the town pond that had been frozen over for several weeks? Walking with great strides on frozen snow, it seemed wonderful that he finally dared venture among ordinary joyous people once again. At the beginning he didn't feel particularly good. He was no longer used to the noise and chatter and above all the laughter. In the past he had always wondered how it was people learned to laugh for the first time. Something violently distorted and incomprehensible must have occurred. This cheerful laugh of the harmless was surely only the poor misguided remnant of a deep tremor among prehistoric people in which excessive pain and pleasure could not be separated. Soon an unusually peaceful and gentle feeling entered him although sadness certainly did not want to leave him. How did this lonely person find this exuberant young group? Looking around the ice rink, he saw he was almost the oldest. Maybe the clumsiest too. But it didn't bother him. Once when he fell to the ground after hitting a rut, he had the bizarre idea that he couldn't imagine Christ on skates. At that, he laughed bitterly then discarded the thought. Do you really have to retreat to the desert to bring about great things? Loneliness is also possible among people. He made great strides on the ice throwing himself into the corners and into clusters of human beings as he mused: if the ice cracked and all the people fell in, what would be the lot? And if all mankind plunged into the earth and then into the sun, what would be left then? What then? *Was für ein unendlicher Zweck wäre für immer geschwunden?*

Then the eternal purpose would vanish forever.

And who would grieve? A spectator and sublime viewer of everything? Or the total thing in itself? Was origin and progress and ending, means, purpose, action and enjoyment unquestionably one and the same with the? And when everything — all things under heaven falls even the sparrows die! At that point he interrupted his investigation half smiling. I must meet thoughts with action now! I must go home and think practically how to contact people and share my thoughts. Yes, what is it you want, fool? The best that a man has cannot find clear words. That will come. Perhaps it's already there, inside me. I only need to mine it. I must begin to speak. My tongue is suddenly loosened. Yes, I've been silent long enough. I just need to start talking. Then it will flow from my lips like a stream of fire. I just have to take that first step.

The time was now. He scrambled to the bench creating a stir among the youth behind him, quickly unfastened his skates and hurried home choosing the closest route through the city. On the way he noticed blue, white and red posters on various street corners. Citizens and schoolchildren stood reading eagerly despite the grim cold. Thoughtless curiosity or perhaps an awakened interest made Starkblom stop. He read on the placard the following: Attention Fellow Citizens! The legislative elections are nearing. This is the most important election in our history.

It seemed to go on for some time and in the end, it was asked to stand up for the tried and tested candidate so and so and to convene a meeting for the following day, Tuesday, January 23rd. Starkblom decided to attend and see what was being done and to get to know the way people did things. Starkblom had previously subscribed to a newspaper when the district judge and his wife were still alive. His deceased wife had a habit of collecting the reports perhaps because she believed that these things could become interesting in later years or maybe only be used to sell the bales of waste. Starkblom had kept the big box in the attic which the housekeeper pulled down and he read on Monday evening and Tuesday. In preparing to meet voters, he read the newspapers thinking it was the best thing to do. He wanted to compare the politician's messages from a several years past. Were they talking the same way today?   It was nasty work reading through the rotten, yellow news of yesteryear, but he grinded his way through it. Of course, he hadn't shaken his head nearly as much as he did now.

The gathering began as if nothing had changed in the political world. There gathered around 800 more or less well-fed citizens who listened carefully without interrupting their speakers. They spoke of grain tariffs and increases in bread prices, free trade and free competition, militarism and the heavy burdens on the people's shoulders, export premiums on sugar and the favoritism toward agriculture and other edifying things. The people appeared to accept the distributions of burdens and the politicization along with moderate dissatisfaction as a natural human right. 'They must be shaken out of it', thought Starkblom.

One would need to approach them with reason and profound reflection. Despair would instill in them a lust for death. He wondered, why was this? The people for their part were so comfortable with their vegetative-like state — and why? Well why not? And if it's so out of malice, that's what I want to do! Why do they need to remain voiceless animals when I am not? What is their lot to me if I am disgusted with it? Why should they be left as they are when human words can transform them? If I have power over them, I want to use it! Why and for what purpose? No more questions. Because I am inclined; it will be my joy! His new thoughts unsettled him, and like the creaking of an old door, it spoke new things to him. The crowd listened more attentively than before. Now and then one would nod their head in agreement. Suddenly, the spirit of freedom seemed to throw off a mask exposing the struggle which rose from below against the regime — perhaps as a temporary joke. They represented the prosperous middle class with power in their hands who above all sought to defend themselves against the covetous poor who demanded the impossible. The Social Democrats baited the uneducated masses who believed in them like new prophets of long-gone utopias. These preachers of revolution had become a danger to the fatherland and educated persons in all countries; above all they fought. Freedom itself offers true economic independence of the individual; it is in him alone that the salvation of the future blooms. Misled workers, say goodbye to the lies of social democracy. A big round of applause greeted the speaker, but the clapping hands drowned out the derisive laughter that emanated from a small group locked in the corner. Another speaker, lean and bony, lifted the mask even more. Or had he himself put on a new one? Freedom had once again become pious. At first, he talked about nature and the struggle on all sides and against Darwin. Suddenly, the word 'God' came up. Starkblom listened with amazement and disgust. God created the world so that everyone had the same rights, but not the same gifts but the same character and happiness. The contradictions between rich and poor, hardworking and lazy, clever and stupid could not be eradicated. Again, he heard bitter laughter. And the inheritance? A screaming voice asked, is it only the clever that inherit the world? Yes, very well and good of the state that the children feed off their father's gifts. It is the family that is the basis of the state and civilization.

During this speech a worker came from the corner and whispered something into the chairman's ear. He looked at the man doubtfully and shrugged. The other made a slight hand gesture. The chairman spread out his arms questioningly. Then he struck the table angrily. The bell echoed a trembling tone and the chairman reluctantly acquiesced the floor. After loud applause subsided, he announced that an opposition speaker wished to address the free discussion. He hoped the patience of the assembly wouldn't be burdened for long.

Now came the worker, a middle-aged man with a serious unflinching expression. He held a long a broad felt hat in his left hand which he waved in a lively yet steady way as we spoke. He looks like he's chopping wood someone whispered and laughed out loud at the joke. The man wasn't a terribly good or bad speaker. He mixed in whimsical and dry commentary with some flowery trivialities. His intention was not to convince anyone because that was not possible. Rather he sought to give his opinion so that it might be known what the worker thought. The light of reason had risen in the proletarian brain and that was to the credit of social democracy. This was the people's heart, a fixed goal which seeks to please all mankind. What good then is your God when he leaves us to our misery? We have turned away from him; you can keep him for yourself. This will be so long as Capitalism lasts and wage slavery endures; therefore, capitalist society must be annihilated completely. All people have the same materials needs; Is it possible to eat more than one lunch? No? Then it is also ridiculous that one fights to get the most money from another. Wherever possible the production of food must be done in common. The struggle of everyone against everyone must stop — here you'll find your vaunted freedom. The wealthy may enjoy freedom but the rest of us are left free to starve and be enslaved; then the freedom will stand by itself. You once fought for the cause of oppressed people when you were oppressed, but now that your stomachs are full you betray the cause the people! But we don't need you anymore. We are proletarians with a purpose standing on the floor of the class struggle and we shall not leave it alone until the sun in the East rises and unleashes class conflict. He delivered his reproach at the end, looking hard at the assembly and a few comrades in the corner: His comrades cheered 'Up', 'Up', 'Up' as he announced 'Long live the international revolutionary social democracy. A certain harmony rose from the rage and din of the congregation.

Starkblom felt elevated by something unheard of. He rose and watched as the workers kept their hats on in protest. He heard the chairman's voice again speaking of the outrageous, provocative behavior. He had had enough and wanted to leave. He exited the side door. As he was closing the door he heard, "Mr. Wangaus, the manufacturer, has the floor." He laughed. So, he wanted to refute the previous speaker, he thought. Oh, this speech he already knew for they all speak the same way. God puts everything in its rightful place! Be contented and don't shake the traditional order of society. Our whole great culture depends on it. But he wanted to shake it and so did the workers. Of course, these workers weren't standing with him. They just wanted to live and start a proper happy life. The happy life? They were being played. There was no happiness in life. If these naïve people had gained everything, luck, wealth, independence, education, and knowledge — they would be more miserable than they are now. Or they would be cattle like those citizens inside there. Or was there a third way? He couldn't believe it. Oh, if only he could believe it! Belief in the future. To a destiny of man, some kind of purpose, a meaning and yet everything so nonsensical, futile and so joyless and ridiculous. They had become like children. They would believe in and enjoy life as long as they lived and conquer the paradise of humanity. Had he not said this? Why the need to enjoy things over and over again? I couldn't enjoy this because I question it; and if I stop and rebel and ponder then finally doubt and despair: am I not an animal?

— And why don't you want to be an animal? Missing being a cheerful being filled with abundance and strength, high spirits and audacity, always plunging into new depths and coming up again to pure heavenly ether and the sounds of bells. And the joy of discerning, always discerning; to be rooted in the earth yet rise up to a be a God, would that not be sublime beauty? Yes, that would be beautiful! Yes, there is work — striving towards a goal, enlightenment, preaching, ennoblement? Fighting? Finding comrades? Perhaps finding fellow believers among the Social Democrats? Yes? Wasn't those the right people for him in the end? They seemed to have a firm, immoveable goal. They wanted something; and wasn't it beautiful and magnificent? And was it not possible? O, it must be possible if there is to meaning in life. And didn't this make sense since he wanted to live and be happy and have hope? And if the people could think of something and want it couldn't this also be fulfilled?   Of course, the philosophers denied this; but wasn't this just —? Anything reasonable is possible; otherwise the reasonable is in truth very unreasonable. Well then let's at least try. Bring on my reason and you my life! We want to test you again. Here stands reason and their life.   If you both don't get together while I'm watching you, I'll throw both of you into the water. You can drown and perish together. Then the little observer enters the realm of death. So, I start. I will attempt it.   I'll have to get to know the Social Democrats.   In the end, I'll become one myself. They'll need me and so the circle will be completed. The height has met the depth and connects with it. One turns away from life so long that he begins a new one.   From a life of disgust! Wasn't it just this life under these circumstances and conditions? And all my disgust and despair, was it just the fruit of my surroundings and my time?   Were new conditions created? Throw away the vague philosophy that is hostile to the individual? Do national economies and histories live? Do they become Social Democrats? Do they fight for institutions and no longer for the people?   Do they cancel relationships and no longer serve the self? They know and no longer understand? Believe and longer despair? Experience happiness and not deep pain? Life and not death? Is this what it means to become a Social Democrat?

His thoughts kept coming back again and again and here he stopped. He laid down and fell asleep and woke to the same thoughts.

When he went a few days later to a Social Democratic reading club "Mankind" and his whole being was a fertile field. He hadn't made a new decision nor had he thought deeply about it or studied anything about social conditions and materialistic history but he was ready to plunge into something new with all the passionate fire that had accumulated in him over time. He found comrades who could lead in achieving the goal in the struggle.

He stepped into the bar shortly before 8 o'clock and the great room was still pretty empty. Half an hour later groups of workers sat around the tables. When the meeting opened shortly after 9 A.M the hall was overfilling with people along the walls and between the tables. Women could be seen here and there. Starkblom sat at a table in the middle of the room, the only stranger in the amidst of over a thousand workers. Shortly before the meeting, two well-dressed young men, evidently merchants had paced back and forth in the hall, scrutinizing and uncertain. Then one said to the other, 'come on'. Nathan, we have to go, nobody is here. A worker who was standing nearby turned around calmly, grabbed the one on the left and the other on the right and pushed them through the door with a hard shove. Starkblom, who had been watching the scene laughed heartily and nodded in a friendly way to the young man who passed by him again. He sat with him and talked about political and scientific matters. It was the first pleasant close conversation Starkblom had in a long while.

Now the speaker was given the floor. He continued on the theme "How are we to vote?" He was still a young man, probably no more than 26 years old who had recently appeared in public in Berlin. He moved from city to city in order to agitate for his cause and arouse the working masses with a new sense of purpose and new energy.

Comrades, the Congressional elections are just around the corner, so he too began the innumerable appeals and speeches that bombarded the masses all over Germany. But only in jest because he immediately went on: what do we care about these elections? Are we to believe these seducers who speculate on our stupidity and the excitement of this time, our weal and woe depending on the ballot we pitch into the ballot box and on the MP, we send to Berlin?

Do we workers believe that we need a representative to get what we want? No, I say this is wrong. We want to help ourselves.

It is false to believe that the universal right to vote that we were given a few decades ago is a concession by the government to the so-called sovereignty of the people. On the contrary, this was a clever way to paralyze the revolutionary movement of free spirits through lies and seduction with the help of the uncomprehending masses, and the participation in political power by ambitious demagogues who present themselves as representatives and who bait and play the people and turn themselves into government cronies. Is it not customary to understand a parliamentary tone to be a certain slick, polite, hypocritical and thoroughly mendacious manner of speaking and appearing? Is it not concerning that in all so-called Parliaments the fine, feeble, so-called aristocratic people who take no responsibility and speak with a common tongue which avoids unevenness and coarseness and yet plays the main role in everything? What if it were even pretended even by those who mean it honestly, if parliament were really the home of free speech where one could say what one thinks is good with impunity in questions of religion, nationality, race, social life, morality, and in all questions as mentioned? What if men had courage of conviction and represented with fiery eloquence what they really thought or dimly felt but is forbidden by so-called "law". Then we would not have anything against Parliament even though it didn't have the meaning many often attribute to it. But where in the world is it like this? On the contrary. Aren't our representatives more fearful of the President's call to order or the mood of the other MPs — their valued colleagues — more than they are of the criminal judge? Don't these men who stand before the echo of the masses speak with more courage and truthfulness? Or do they lie there with their free speech as much as the fine words of the parliamentarians? The woe to these representatives and leaders! They have been betrayers and bought traitors! The so-called constitutional state, a form of unification, a compromise of the feudal, medieval government, of Junkerism, kingship setting God's grace on one side and civil society on another. So long as the struggle was between the bourgeois and the feudal world, our place was on the side of the bourgeoisie; back then we were still too weak to fight both at the same time or be a laughable third party they stood there while they quarreled. Today, however, this fight is only a sham. On this day one single view of life no longer fights against another, but *it is only one interest against another interest.* Only we who are strong in unity and in our new view of life must unite our opponents by fighting against both of them. We will leave them their state and their capitalist institutions, their church and their parliament — we will stand outside of it all. As we now stand outside in a place where need compels us to labor for the sake of wages, so then we will stop working all at once at the time of our choosing when the time is right. The speaker who had spoken with fire in his words accompanied by strong movements of his arms and hand was interrupted by thunderous applause. Starkblom listened intently. He was in the right place. We could stop working whenever we wanted. That was the situation. Of course, everything was in another context. Nothing in opposition to life rather everything for the sake of life, for the rational life. That was what these men were so sure of: there was a reason in life, and a future. There was joy and purpose and an interest in the world, and one's descendants. One acted and made sacrifices for the cause and goal in which one believed. This was what he longed for with all his being. These men knew what they lived for and what they would die for. Starkblom endeavored to destroy any doubts that seemed to come from all sides. He didn't want to be unhappy anymore. He wanted to participate and he let himself be carried away in the moment no matter where it took him.

The speaker took a sip of beer and began again.

The question that concerns us about the elections has widened: What do we have to do with politics? Are we, as proscribed, a political party or are we something else, something bigger? What is politics then? In German they call it statecraft. That's correct. Without the state there is no diplomacy and no parliament and no politics. How in the devil does the state improve the social order today? It is wrong to think we can sneak in through states back door and achieve our goal. It is false to believe that this little door in parliamentarianism was left open accidentally or out of necessity; On the contrary. Today's rulers have opened it wide to lure us and educate us to be docile state donkeys and there is a great danger that this will be achieved.

Comrades, we are not a political party. We aren't interested in making laws to restore order to conflicts of interests and to suppress the weak and secure the rich; we don't want to mend today's world to make it more bearable, no. I'll be frank. We want to make it unbearable in order to accelerate its demise. We know no contradiction between individual nations and we are all one as proletarians in the fight against capital. We wish for all people to become one and as individuals join in the fight against natural forces and in the fight for progress and culture! Once again; we don't want to take part in societies processes, we want to stand aside. We want to leave today's society alone and at the right time, let it go.

In order to achieve this, we turn mainly to the individual. We say to him: Look brother, you have no duty to the state or the so-called community. There is also no duty against God. All of this told you is a lie. What you do and believe has only to do with your reason. This is ensured by the common descent of all people that despite all inequalities and differences they have only one reason and a normal mind is at least able to grasp the greatest things discovered by the most advanced and ingenious. Admittedly, we must clear away a jumble of superstition and nonsense and lies beforehand. Capitalist thinking has been grafted onto the worker, but fortunately it does not coincide with the workers interest in the long run. So it is that the bulk of the working class may well understand every new great idea. This does not apply to the bourgeoisie — you can preach reason all day long and the average bourgeoisie won't agree with us, even if he is honest. If a bourgeoisie is to be convinced of an idea that adheres to a new world view, then he must be a free person who knows how to rise above the interests of his own class. And those are few. But what workers among us does not understand when I say: you pay taxes, soldier, labor in the factory not because you want to but because you are enslaved because those who subjugate you are still stronger for the time being. As individuals you can stop working, but you will starve. If you rebel against state and moral laws that don't concern you, then you will be deprived of your freedom or killed outright by law because law is power. You can leave off everything that you don't wish to do. But under the weight of bondage, you cannot do what you want. You cannot satisfy your educational instinct, or create a dignified existence for yourself. You cannot rid yourself of things that disgust you like fraudulent stock deals, prostitution, lying clergy and perfidious officialdom or the wrong associated with the destruction of the education of the youth. In short, you cannot live as you wish. Your living conditions are dictated by the conditions of want which are maintained and defended and idealized by today's bourgeoisie society.

In these circumstances there is only one remedy. All who suffer must these conditions must come together to form a fighting community. We will not cease teaching reason and enlightening the people until we have achieved the unification of all proletarians of all countries to overthrow the capitalist worldview and establish a socialist one. Let us organize in the trade unions, place our program in the factories, on the streets, inside each family and at large gatherings. If this free organization is strong enough, then each individual group can support each other in the struggle for improvement in living conditions, a reduction in working hours and an increase in wages. Then every single group can temporarily quit bourgeoisie society if only to give a taste of what's to come. This fighting organization must reflect the future of the society. Each stakes his life and property for with the other to achieve the same goal; one for all and all for one.

Citizens, do not participate in the vote for the Congress. Do not choose another talking head in the parliament. Words are not for struggle, but for instruction and there can be no representatives needed for the fight. Fight for yourselves proletarians. Not with your mouths, but fight with your whole person. Fight where it needs to be taken. On the shop floor where you cannot fight alone, fight together, firmly united. Unite proletarians, enlighten with your ideas Comrades and victory will be ours! Again, there was uproarious clapping and energetic shouts of approval drowning out the "quite wrong" spoken by an isolated person. The discussion now opened. One worker after another stepped forward to express as best, he could his approval for the proceedings and level serious accusations at the representatives of the people. The lone opponent now had his say in fluent and eloquent speech he called the accusations unjust saying the leaders deserved merit and that parliament was made for argumentation and should be preserved. The speaker responded by stating that many considered it incorrect that the bourgeoisie represented by parliament had made concessions to us by allowing us to send a number of representatives to that body. This is false, I say. Concessions were made (though they are not really so) because the masses have become too large and dangerous and something had to be done. The ruling class needed to be aware if the injustice of the situation and now wants a remedy for it.

How much stronger and energetic would the socialist movement be today had we not spent our agitation efforts on elections and instead oppose parliament from the start.[3] I maintain the gentleman in the Reichstag and at the green tables would have felt a completely different sense of horror and made more decisive concessions if socialist had never entered their meeting room. Perhaps they needed to hear the voices penetrating from the outside from working people who want nothing in common with them. What do these gentleman care if a smooth speaker dabbles in this and that, always asking for a modest amount from the gentlemen? And how different the Reichstag negotiations would have been if the bourgeoise gentleman had stayed just among themselves wasting time on foolish insensitive chatter and day long arguments about formalities and trivialities. All this while outside the workers join together tighter and tighter and struggle for bread and the reorganization of humanity (rather than fighting against the grain tariffs)! As columns of workers gathered in the galleries whispering excitedly, they began to speak out as the bourgeoisie gentleman cringed in the corner with fear. Have you ever seen the people speak to MPs like this? No. Most listened carefully and then praised the oratorical performance.

---

[3] This was a common lesson derived from the European struggles of 1848/49. Ferdinand Lasalle 1825-1864 wrote a letter to Marx in 1849 "The experiences of Austria, Hungary and Germany in 1848 and 1849 have led me to the firm conclusion that no struggle in Europe can be successful unless it is proclaimed from the very beginning as purely Socialistic."

That must change. In this way our movement must spread out more and more. Let us not strain ourselves just yet; Let us be careful to ensure the masses do not tire and lose faith in our cause. Dissatisfaction, and the passion for radical change must not disappear. It must increase. The enlightenment and instruction must unite together. Take care! Let us stand shoulder to shoulder! And above all: We do not wish to vote, but we protest against the vote! In the midst of the storm of applause which rose again some were preparing to leave as the great crowd sat quietly in expectation of the third item: "Miscellany" on the agenda which interested Starkblom who now stood up. A thought had occurred to him in the last half hour *'You must keep repeating the single word: talk, talk, talk.' There should be no more silence.'* He shivered and sweat stood on his forehead. Something pressed his throat. Now as he stood mute, he couldn't shake the fever and the anxiety. The chairman asked "Does anyone want the floor?" Starkblom stretched his arm up as he had seen others. The following thoughts raced in his head: Now you must speak; you must. But what to say? He doesn't know what to say. And the thoughts ran ahead, now's the time, say something meaningful.

"It's your turn," said the voice at the podium. "Name, address, step forward," said the chairman quickly. Starkblom stepped forward. He composed himself, but couldn't focus. He kept repeating 'Gentlemen, gentlemen', moving his lips. But as he reached the front he said calmly to the police lieutenant who was watching the meeting: Karl Starkblom, Villa White House, private citizen.

"You have the floor," repeated the chairman among some confusion in the meeting; the people were eager to hear what the man had to say. Starkblom began speaking fluent words, calmly and only pausing briefly between individual sentences when he drew a deep breath because of the excitement in his chest. "Gentlemen, the first speaker was correct." A free and exceptional person is required in order for one of the ranks of the educated to rise above his surroundings that kept him from an early age. Even if he is free and with special mettle, life may turn out very differently from assumptions. If chance plays a trick and keeps him away from people who think differently and never let him get together with people whose thoughts travel in a completely different direction. I am no longer young, but I am in the presence of workers for the first time in my life. I am not a bourgeoisie in the sense you use it. Unawares, I have in life thoughtlessly adopted today's customs and morality. In my long struggle, I rose completely above everything that I had ever been taught save one thing I never knew until now: there are people who feel and think very differently than we do up there and that the future can lie in the hands of these people. I mastered the lessons of my time; I have watched all life and events on this earth. I've seen how people meander and let themselves be pushed by any chance. They have no goal, no inner reflection and I turned away with disgust from the human race that seems not to know what it lives for — and worse — does not even want to know. I was close to stepping away from humanity because after much searching, I could not find what I was living for. I had the courage in my thoughts to at least draw conclusions from my life and this is the case for all those in my social circle. The consequence has been this: suicide.

I can say today that the bourgeois world has fallen to it death. From its ruins I hope together a socialist society and new world will rise. At this point, the heretofore large assembly dissolved into a polyphonic and simultaneous cheer. Starkblom wiped his forehead lightly and took a deep breath; then he spoke again, now more lively and joyful as if infected by the sympathy of the assembly. "Gentlemen, it's now clearer than ever and we can build on this. What disgusts me most in my deepest soul is not humanity or even the world itself. It is the people who I grew up with and have spent my whole life; it is in the *conditions* that prevail today, handed down to every child and drawing them into the endless cycle of rotten living. But I know one child who has not yet been ruined by these institutions; a field that has not yet been weeded with the plow of old morals and is ready for new seed; a cloud that has not yet broken open, but is filled with fresh, life-giving rain; a wheel whose unbroken rim has just begun to roll who knows where? ... I am speaking of the working class. You did not enjoy the education which stuffed our brains, but gave you space for new ideas. You are called to deliver the fatal blow to the old rotten society and replace it with new reason where unreason reached the end of its development. Our foolish bourgeois society believed that it was allowed to give the people a certain degree of will and enlightenment. They cannot get rid of the spirits they conjured up. Society could have been sustained if workers had been systematically made into farm animals, or worse still, factory animals; but in a fit of sentimental stupidity with a reminiscence of the human rights of the French Revolution, they shrank from it and wanted to plug their spirits with half measures. Lo and behold, the spirit in them was awakened and faster than they expected it grew into a new, great revolution much more powerful than the so-called great revolution of the bourgeoisie. Workers have a new belief, a belief in themselves and the future of humanity. The civil society; however, has no faith – old or new. Where it has not regressed into a thoughtless morass and become live a farm animal, it has sunk into despair. This social revolution will succeed!

A huge applause broke out. Starkblom sensed the audience and although he could have continued, he added a few more things through the din. Those who were desperate about the future of the bourgeois society and yet believe mankind had more to offer flocked to them: they asked to be admitted into the ranks believing that they shared the same burning desire: the rational design for human life!

Starkblom wanted to leave the podium and exit the hall as quickly as possible. He desired to make his way into the fresh air and return home. We wondered how he could have spoken even a single word now. The chairman standing next to him tapped him on the shoulder and said, "Thank you very much, Mr. Starkblom. If you would only wait a bit. We're almost finished here. Would you be so kind?" Starkblom shook his hand and said, "Certainly." During this brief conversation everyone had risen and ran in great confusion towards the exit. In keeping with form, the chairman asked "Is there anyone wishing a word?" He then quickly closed the meeting to the rising strains of the Workers Marseillaise: [4] *Wohlan, wer Recht und Wahrheit achtet, zu unsrer Fahne steh allzuhauf!–* as more people joined in the refrain while pushing for the exit. Only a few struggled against the surging crowd. When the hall emptied, seven men stood before Starkblom. He nodded in all directions saying yes – yes – quite right, but please. He really couldn't hear the others and he himself didn't know what he was saying. He could have stood there for hours in the excitement. A man roused him and asked they sit at a table and have another beer. Soon Starkblom was involved in a conversation with his new friends. At first, they spoke about indifferent subjects and his life outside the city. Soon they were drawn into a conversation developing on the other side of the table. They talked about the conditions and divisions within the German Social Democratic Party. Starkblom learned that the revolutionary tendency was not as strong in other places; in other places the masses were

---

[4] The German Worker Marseillaise is a song written in 1864 by Jacob Audorf for the General German Workers' Association to the melody of the Marseillaise. It begins:
Come all who respect law and truth,
to our flag that is so high!

content with buzzwords and left everything to their adored leaders. "Yes, but these leaders, and the people who seem sensible and enthusiastic, can they really believe that the great goal can be achieved through traditional political means and parliamentary work? This is quite unthinkable." "Let me explain something to you," said Mathis Buvolski an official who had previously presented on elections. "These gentlemen are very clever which is their undoing. Hopefully not ours. They don't really believe in the power of the movement and especially not in the power of enlightenment. They give great speeches about economic development and that socialist society is self-made. There is no need to get involved and put yourself in danger. But they don't want to give up power. They await some special event, a great coincidence, preferably a revolution from above, a breach of the constitution by the government. And so that the movement doesn't come to a standstill or even melt away, they use artificial means to keep it alive. So, there is a great storm of indignation all over Germany over grain tariffs, only with the intent of generating mass gatherings all over the place. "What?" Starkblom interrupted. "I heard the same thing from the Liberals a few days ago."

"Yes, but that doesn't matter. We have more to offer. And it is the same reason that there must be elections and members speeches and endless motions. A new project pops up every few weeks with proposals to impress the masses of people, the nationalization of pharmacies, healthcare, the grain trade ... The movement is everything and cannot be allowed to sleep. But nothing is done, no serious explanations given either verbally or in writing. The provincial newspapers are terrible, the magazines too expensive and the leaders in the assembly have no time to instruct the people. They make names for themselves and stay on top, so when the time comes, they can have power in their hands. This is why there is no unanimity and constant bickering and jealousy."

"What are we talking about?" interjected Starkblom. "They are ordinary people, not without talent, but ordinary. What does this have to do with people? There is more to socialism than today's purveyors probably even suspect. What do we care about these petty details when it comes to the future of humanity?"

The others listened intently, but Buvolski spoke, "You spoke well and warmly and with solemnity this evening. But I have yet met anyone willing to do what everything possible to turn what he believes into reality. Is it not a fact that you believe in the power of reason?"

Starkblom felt the color drain from his face. He felt a chill up his spine. If, if ... if. There was no 'if'. He shook himself. He would take nothing from the past. He didn't want it anymore. He believed in his decision. Only after a pause, with everyone looking at him, did he answer: "That's quite a lot. I don't believe I am alone. To be honest, I don't quite understand what you are saying."

"I am a part of the world, just a small part, perhaps scattered and lonely, it's true. That I am rational, well that I know for certain; I believe I have not risen above this world so far that it can no longer follow me. A person can do a lot if they choose; the Will can be awakened. The mind of a man is so arranged that when one has used all the pain and despair of a lifetime to achieve one thing, he can spare others this hardship by understanding the finished result of his life power. In this sense, every great person is a Savior who takes the pain of the world and is crucified to redeem the world." "— where do you live, can you give me your address?" They stared at him in wonder. He stood up. "I can't stay here any longer. It won't be our last meeting, I'm sure."

Buvolski told him where he lived and Starkblom asked the men to visit him soon time willing, and after a warm farewell, he left. He hurried home. As long as he was on the city streets, he walked quickly, drew in air and smiled to himself. He swung his stick occasionally hitting the stone slabs which caused sparks to fly. On the country roads with freshly fallen snow his gaze wandered onto the fields whose immeasurable blanket of snow glittered in the moonlight. He began to run as if to race his own shadow. He screamed Juhu, juhu! An indescribable joy seized him. Now he wasn't thinking at all or brooding about the future. He had something in the present to be happy about. He surrendered himself to the feeling of enjoyment as thoughtlessly as a child.

He was near his village when he met a young girl. She called to him in the distance. "Have they released you?" Starkblom immediately understood her and laughed until he stood in front of her. She thought of the town madhouse where incurable people were locked up from all over the country. "Well not exactly," he replied cheerfully. "Maybe I'll get that far. Nice night eh?" He looked happily at in the face of the pretty young woman. "What do you mean?" She asked somewhat embarrassed adjusting the handkerchief she wore on her head. "Well, I think there is only one reason a girl is out here so late. Is he handsome? Is he honest? "I don't know," she said blushing a little. "I just like him."

"You are right. That explains everything. What does he do for work?"

"He works in a factory."

"Ah, is he a Social Democrat then?"

"Well, I told you he works in a factory."

"Ah, yes, that's right."

"How long have we been on a first name basis?"

"Only for today, young lady. I don't mean to offend, it's just that I've been so happy today."

"Well, I am happy for you too. I like funny people."

"I hadn't been this way for some time."

"Oh?"

"Yes, for some time."

Yes, you seem troubled and sad. Stay happy, it's better."

"I'll try. Can I have a kiss?" "No, or Yes, because you are special." She lay her hand on his shoulder and he kissed her quickly. Then she gave him several more kisses, shook his hand and turned to go.

"Goodbye happy Sir, don't think anything badly of me."

"Be well young lady and give regards to your love."

He clicked his tongue a few times out of happiness. He slowly climbed the mountain stopping a few times to let his gaze wander over the fields, woods and river which lay in whiteness over the city before him. He stretched out his arm and moved his hand as if in blessing and thanks. Smiling, he looked out onto the road and saw a dark point in the far distance. Once more energy broke through his chest and he loudly cried out in joy once again. And he heard the girl's soft answer. He nodded and smiled to himself then unlocked the door and went up to his bedroom and turned on the light. He became serious and paced back and forth a bit while grumbling to himself: yes, yes. Then he undressed, turned off the light and tried to sleep. After a few minutes he fell asleep.

From that day on, Karl Starkblom became a passionate supporter and herald of socialism. He soon gained influence over the people, wrote brilliant pamphlets, travelled around the country and gave lectures in large public places and in small societies as well as in professional associations. He became one of the most passionate fighters against bourgeois society — and he did not forego the use of reason and conviction to win over the most advanced elements for his cause. He seemed completely absorbed in this activity and knew what he was living for. Perhaps the thing was he had no time to ponder.

But one evening — he had been busy for months — something strange happened. Of course, when he thought about it later, the idea had appeared now and again as a sudden pang of doubt which left quickly enough. In truth, he hadn't paid much attention to it. At the meeting he had experienced an anxiety that made him nauseous. It happened on one evening before he went to sleep and again another time. There was no context, rather it was like a sudden shudder a dumb thought quickly forgotten again.

This time; however, it overwhelmed him. He gave a lecture on the subject to an extraordinarily well attended meeting in a large city in western Germany: "Why Must Socialism Win?" The hall was stifling hot and the air terribly bad; A storm raged outside. In the first part of the speech he painted the present state of human society in stark terms. Lately, he has failed to carefully prepare for his speeches; He want to be carried away by a flood of thoughts and words. He entered a new train of thought. It didn't bother him and he continued but was careful to suppress any second thoughts. He spoke of the great difference that existed in fighting for a socialist society and reaching it and the current state of society. This would be a transitional stage to the second part, a broad outline of the socialist society. But he couldn't get over the thought. He knew what to do. He finished the sentence, then paused. Then the new thoughts would come to him naturally. But this time it happened differently. As soon as he waited a few seconds, an inward rebellion took hold and a horrible secondary thought remained unshakable. "Give it up, it's all wrong! There is no point in anything! It whirled inside his head. "Nothing makes sense!" "Totally false! Oh, give it all up!" He braced himself against the table and struggled to finish. "Gentlemen," he began violently. "In considering the second part of my argument ..." Then he fell silent.

"Stop it. It's a lie. Think about the other things first – there's no point in it. What do other people concern you?" He screamed then raised his hands to his head and collapsed. The meeting broke up with great commotion. When Starkblom came to, he felt miserable. The next morning, he went back to his house. There he passed time alone and silent for a long time. A few months later a small pamphlet appeared which caused quite a stir in literary and political circles. It was titled, "A Letter From Karl Starkblom to the human race: A Rejection of Socialism."

PART 3

Letter from Karl Strakblom to the human race.

At the same time the rejection of socialism occurred, there was a note in the social democratic provincial newspaper. It read, "the well-known agitator Dr. Starkblom still does not seem to have recovered from his regrettable illness and cannot take up his work again for the time being."

It was true that the disease that attacked me struck once more and did not subside. The disease now assumed an epidemic character; I felt the maddening desire to infect my fellow peaceful human beings if only to free myself from the tormenting awareness that other people are very healthy and that it was only I that had been cast out of the beautiful community.

Perhaps it's the other way around? Yes, that must be it. You are upset and I — well I am more upset than you I suppose. But I want to infect you in my madness if only to make myself appear healthy. Because illness is only a contradiction and an expulsion of the individual from the community.

Now I want to talk about that. I want to say that socialism is a matter for mediocre and ordinary natures. I want to withdraw with those who understand me from a community of comrades who relate to me and my teachings.

By socialism, I mean the preconditions it makes without admitting them to itself and others although it would be wise and old enough to understand. It exists under the spell of old words and it is not able to speak a single new word. Socialism, although it finds good in a new worldview, presupposes that there is an obligation for man to look after his neighbors and that there is a community of men and that the individual has an interest in the future of humanity and the world. It never justifies this most important prerequisite because it is completely under the spell of morality, the Judeo-Christian moral law and its variations and because it is unable to even suspect the possibility of a new worldview and soulview. Socialism is not original, rather a series of historical reminiscences. When it speaks revolution, it means what has hitherto been understood as revolution. It knows no other ways and means than those which have apparently been effective up until now. Socialism is shameless because it believes in itself. It is childish because it does not think of death.

Socialism is pathetic because it lets itself be ruled by an abstract idea. It is a poor thing because it does not know a rich life. Socialism is an imaginary sick man who keeps making his wills instead of living or just giving up the ghost. It is a lie because it talks about the future and is superstitious while it claims the mantle of science.

One wants proof of these things. You didn't ask for it. I don't wish to prove it. I am not a prosecutor or examining magistrate. I only give my impressions and experiences. I abhor the screaming tone of unconditionality. But, I love the obvious. If you take many things for granted, follow me. If you haven't gotten used to the agitation and the for and against, then just stay where you are. The best way to find people like me is to avoid them and keep walking. You become mature. And I only wish to speak to mature people. Are you too tired? Words have become indifferent to me. And the world too? Yes, the world too. There is only one thing left of importance to me, worth thinking about and waiting for. I am happy as a thief at this inconsistency. The one thing is — and you may laugh my friends — the one thing is death. He is close to my heart and I still have a lot to tell him. Are you ready? I wish then to tell you something — about life.

Wait, shouldn't I talk about my life and thoughts in the past and a bit about my innermost processes and moods — shouldn't I speak about the economic conditions and nail down the incontrovertible truth from the outset that material phenomenon produces ideas and that all my thoughts and opinions are the fruits of our age of capitalism?   Should I be organized differently than by God and law. Before speaking of myself, shouldn't I observe and determine how things happen and where history goes according to the immanent economic laws of Karl Marx?   In short, should I not be a fool?   A fool to whom his own level headed observations are worth more than all his thousandfold accumulated, unconscious and accidental experiences? Shouldn't I always feel like a ring in the chain of fixed development? Shouldn't I divide myself into two parts and let the one rule the other? Shouldn't I join with those who know instead of being one who doesn't want to know, as I am now?

Yes, that's why, to me at least. I feel odd and strange and maybe important: I am one with them – because I am not the only one? — to those who forget everything that should have been there, the ancestral things past and reasonings which no one wants to know anything about. People who are too chaste to live their lives according to knowledge and communication and observation but live instead like divine beasts moving towards an unknown goal. Oh, you persistent and immutable ones, anchored in history and purpose, insightful, jumpers with two feet, living for the future and not in the present, you living high for the moment, conscious simians, versatile and productive, animal killers and God molesters and mutilators, you paper people and wired dolls — you disgust me in the extreme! That Socrates who at least knew what he didn't know wasn't this malodorous. But where do find someone who doesn't want to know anything? Who just wants to live — or die?

So, I want to begin my speech with life. The life of the highest man. I don't want to speak of the needs of life, for the poorest of the poor. I should say I am a hard person, a prince of the earth, above everything that stands below him and far removed from the feeble emotion of pity. But I don't like to pretend or forced consistency. Yes, I feel pity for proletarians, hot pity even, but it is not a comforting feeling. It is a feeling that remains in spite of everything. I refuse to allow it to become the center of all my wishes, views and intentions. You dear ones who only see life from afar in shining splendor and who know life's needs and the appearance of life do not know life. You have the right to fight for life with all your strength and for what you call the enjoyment of life.   I understand you who chase after a beautiful picture and keep chasing until you find bitter disappointment. I can't speak to you early enough. Seek life so that you can learn to flee from it.

But the others, those social democratic teachers and leaders, among them, I think, should be some who could know something about life. If the longing for life grows, it is partly out of stupidity that they tells themselves that the misery of the living soul is based on the same reason as the needs of working children — namely on the economic conditions of the age; or they are ordinary people who endure their lives only by dominating others, but do not understand their humanness. They look at the world through sharp eyes and grasp it scientifically, but have never felt the desire to examine — and despise their own actions and lives. These petty mediocre souls who make life bearable for themselves through their talking — and that's what they call a new worldview! — and who are nothing short of marvelous in their lust for domination and seduction. They don't even know why they're preaching the future, they're foolish enough to believe it's really for the future's sake, these egoists and don't even know it — oh, what's in the heads of children! You strive for something because you love the striving as part of your soul, but they tell themselves that their whole soul is drawn to a Something outside. They do not know that something is only an indifferent and accidental symbol of their inner being. This is projected into the future in order to be more glamorous and to control it! In other times it would have been projected into the heavens! And to some onto the island of Utopia. And a third time on Olympus or in the golden age or in the garden of paradise. They believe that the future is something in reality and that it concerns people more than heaven and hell. O, these children's minds! Again, I must completely separate these leaders from those who have been led and been seduced. I have pity for them admittedly, but there is no contempt from the kind of sympathy. On the contrary, I see the great pain and difficulty of the path that awaits these excellent people until they reach where I stand, until they see their needs which separate them from life. These things must be overcome for in the innermost core of life, of human life, there is an insurmountable and much deeper misery that wears an ugly covering. Of course, it seems to me that in a strange way, socialism would shorten the path in rare cases while in the case of the great masses it completely buries it making it inaccessible and unseen. I know some few people, simple workers, whom I've taken into my heart. For many years they were ardent, dyed in the wool Social Democrats. In their simplicity They saw through the motives of the leaders and saw things in these people that they were not even aware of in their simplicity. It's hard to believe with what strange, terrible speed they — the few — now flew their own way or were torn or smashed. They called themselves socialists when they were no longer so. They were always looking for new and less trodden paths to achieve a "great goal" which they continually searched after; they shake off the doctrine of economic foundation and call themselves idealists and anarchists again. They became individualists, but their own never heard of kind, because they were still looking for individualism in the future as an ideal. They wanted to create individualism through common work, through Communism. But they also demanded that the ways and means must be individualistic. They stripped off their being and wanted nothing more. They were no longer individualists, but individuals. Alone, they succumbed to pessimism. They lost their faith and longing for life. Strange that these chosen people had hardly lived life, hardly seen it really. They had only an inkling of life passing through their souls and they shyly turned away from it. They must be standing there smiling sadly as I tell you about them. Yes, these people are among my listeners and they are in the front row, their hearts open to me, waiting on every word I speak.   When I mention the word "death", it sounds familiar to them; they have softened and understand me. And they follow me. I bless you brothers from different mothers. Now we found one another and shall stay together.

O, these Social Democrats who have seen so much and know everything but nothing of their unconscious will and nothing of their own true natures. These learned little people who live on words and believe a word is a word and a thing a thing. They see all compound things as if it was as simple as taking the opposite for unity.   Because they are happy striving for the future, they believe that happiness in the future is assured when the will of the present is fulfilled.   Little do they know that intention and purpose are two things that never come together. They think they are the same. How unbelievably embarrassed they are when a simple worker whom everything is unconscious and who has almost no desired and controlled knowledge — has clearly recognized this basic truth and whose words burst forth with an incredibly beautiful force: "Freedom, you wonderful word, you signal life and call from another world. How it penetrates my whole being.

You let me fly like an eagle up to a shining hill in the pure air leaving behind all the dust and human misery. Alas the eagle must return to its aerie, as we must return to our human home. You must then sympathize with the thousands who live in unjust fetters and hear the sound of the shackles. You perceive my indignation when I see air and light bound in chains.

Whenever the cry of freedom rings out because of unjust chains, it is the call of the good, the call of reason. Here freedom means goodness; Freedom as strength is not good, for those who put on unjust fetters freedom rules. This is the bad and the reason for the lack of goodness.[5]

Freedom and reason are the two active and combative forces in the individual human being in all races and genders. The more reason dominates speakers and listeners, the more the call to freedom, and with it the call to equality, will disappear. "

One worker who has been less effected by socialism, writes this. Does this shame you? Do you have any idea what you have destroyed and watered down, the depth you lacked and what you have destroyed

---

[5] *Die Freiheit als Kraft ist aber nicht das Gute, vielmehr bei denen, welche ungerechte Fesseln anlegen, herrscht die Freiheit, das ist das Schlechte, und fehlt das Gute, das ist die Vernunft.*

forever?   Don't you see this stammering worker almost laughing at you now?   What could have been achieved had you not been so serious!   What movement could a few big frivolous fellas brought about? If you had talked to the individual and taught him to laugh and die!   What do you all know of laughing and dying?   O, the serious and boring buffoons all the live life long! O, you moral and good folk, so legalistic and economic! O how wrong your socialism is because you wanted it straight ahead, always like some kind of forward march! Because you could only see one thing in front of you, you blinded ones! Your hypnotized, media-fed, mediocrities!

How long do you think you can wait? Has there ever been such maddening blindness like this? You drew some pathetic conclusions from a couple of observations made thirty or more years ago, and now you have grafted them onto your beliefs — O, no, excuse me, an eternal science of economics, really? You formed a party and things have shaped up slowly as prophesized and since the bourgeoisie crumbles ever so slowly you can take your time preaching the same thing, tirelessly. You preach and preach so that in time you will become part of the world's memory. Do you really believe in your infallibility and in your terrible slowness?   Do you really think nothing, absolutely nothing, could grow over your head? Did you have any idea that 30 or 40 years ago, there were voices sounding our bourgeoisie society that had nothing to do with exploitation? Voices like mine, if they are heard and echo, are they not part of your business?   Is the world not quite different from your dreams when a section of the bourgeoisie society laughs at its own shadow and trips over its own blade? If we cancel ourselves, can we still be expropriated?

I hear a voice answer saturated with Marxism and hungry for Kapital, "you and the likes of you are just a phenomenon of decay and corruption." You are isolated bourgeois who are oversaturated and blasé, no can no longer find pleasure. You play no role here. Everything remains as it was. Capitalism exploits, the proletariat starves or at least lives in inhumane conditions — until the hour of liberation strikes. So, it is and shall be!

That is the language of Socialism and some think the man is right.

The man is not right because he does not know the real pain and disgust because he does not know life. Before I give you my opinion of life, I want to share a parable: my friends, do you know the story of the child? It occurs to me that you don't know the story at all; You only know world history and cultural history and other useless falsehoods. You miss the stories of the individual and their changes and ways of looking at things. So now — direct your thoughts to the child, the little child. Do you know how people used to view such a small being? With deep pity because of his helplessness. One regretted that the tiny human did not know life and did not yet understand the enjoyment of life; One spoke of the "poor child". But how is it today? Nobody today says the child is lucky or happy because they don't know life. The child isn't envied. Doesn't everybody look back on their childhood as a time of complete happiness? How about sleep? Nobody knows the history of sleep either. Wasn't going to sleep a fearful thing? Wasn't it a frightening thing to lose consciousness and with it the joy of being? Wasn't a child's fear of helplessness in sleep something to be feared? And now? One looks forward to sleep and smiles before doing so. Losing consciousness is a delight. One does not wish to wake and often falls asleep again a second time in the morning. This is where one dreams only to wake up disturbed and terrified by the light of day the sunshine of life. And what is more terrifying for those living now than a sleepless night. Sleep employs all means possible just to sleep.

Do you still wish to claim that capitalism brings this about, this horror of life and the longing for conditions that really resemble death? No! Away with your guilty conscience and lies and whatever you want to invent. We have pretty good consciouses and are little bothered by exploitation.   There are hundreds and thousands of the noblest and highest people who have lived much further than socialism could ever take them.   They don't care about production and for generations they have lived this way. and always will be despite what you may say. Their families have provided them with all the luxuries of life, they have clear consciences because they don't know anything and don't wish to know anything about your discoveries, the machinery that serves you and is fed into by people — poor, sweating enslaved human children; consequently, they remain untouched by the capitalist institutions. Our choicest thinkers and poets belong to these people who step like gods on the heights over the backs of the working wage slaves. What do they think of life after all? Didn't Goethe tell us that at the end of his life, when all was said and done, that he had only truly been happy for a few hours during the whole of his long life?   Who disbelieves this shocking confession? A few hours! And this was one of the happiest men that ever lived! Whose fanaticism and stupidity are so limitless that it wants to claim that the economic situation is to blame? This can never, ever be true. There is a deeper reason that lies at the root of the whole unfortunate nature of man and life! The reason is that man is a thinking animal and yet will never ever in an entire eternity find a purpose for his existence he can believe in. If someone thinks they've found the purpose, once again they discover there isn't a purpose, nor meaning behind it. Life is again without purpose. And so, it will remain. You can change the economic foundations all you want. When work is no longer necessary and the human is free to do what is good for the body and mind, he may be called a god except on a single point which will always ask the question of purpose: why all this over and over again? And one finds no work forevermore.

Except for one thing, I said. If it weren't for that, he would be a God, a perfect God. A perfect being whose terrible misery would be perfect. If man had to live forever and ask forever 'what for' – O the thought is inconceivable. Let me be silent and happy that it is not so. Yes, there is one thing that people rejoice in and cheer for. They throw themselves deep, deep inside this abyss of laughter, the shining abyss of happiness: this is death. Shout for joy and receive it with open arms by blessed friends. That is death![6] You stand there amazed, my friends. You've always thought something similar, but now I will speak it plainly. Now you are looking for excuses and suddenly want to find a way that could make life worth living? Search as you like and you'll not find anything.

The socialists are fools. They live completely in the struggle for their goal and do not consider that a time will come when their goal is achieved. What then? Well then all will be glorious and joyous. They will have heaven on earth as they always assured us. The word "heaven" means little to me. Let me give you a different description.

Imagine the socialist society is here. You can think of it as having been here for some time and it is fully consolidated. Technology has made tremendous progress. There are no longer unpleasant activities. Children are trained to the highest degree, both physically and mentally. A 15-year-old is a genius

---

[6] Landauer echoes Beat writers like Jack Kerouac who famously wrote in Desolation Angels: Even Hozomeen'll crack and fall apart, nothing lasts, it is only a faring-in-that-which-everything-is, a passing-through, that's what's going on, why ask questions or tear hair or weep, the burble blear purple Lear on his moor of woes he is only a gnashy old flap with winged whiskers beminded by a fool—to be and not to be, that's what we are—Does the Void take any part in life and death? does it have funerals? or birth cakes? why not I be like the Void, inexhaustibly fertile, beyond serenity, beyond even gladness, …

compared to our greatest geniuses who look like poor orphans. Every adult works an hour and a half a day which is enough time for production and distribution of all needs however the requirements may have increased. Technology itself has improved to a much greater extent. Everybody spends the rest of their time doing whatever they want. Friends, do you not believe me when I say that this apparently wonderful state of affairs becomes so wonderful and so habitual that the whole people or nation will surrender to the philosophy that there are no more hardships and struggles with the material games that one has time to think deeply all day and asks: what are we here for? Why do we need this wonderful, complicated apparatus? Are we ends in ourselves? No, that can't be, otherwise we wouldn't need to ask the question. Are we part of some bigger picture in the world? Yes, what is it then we have to do with the world? We have no idea about the joy that she has in our existence, we don't partake in it and are excluded. Then these god-like humans would have to ask themselves over and over again: is there a unity and singularity keeping humanity together? Is there a totality in the real world of all phenomena? O no, you would have to answer. We have long passed such high-level abstractions. The individual human is of course not a conglomerate of individual cells. He is a unit with a consciousness. But what would he be if individual human beings were not dependent on each other? More importantly, what do we have to do with those that come after us? So, when the whole joke is over, after my death, we can ask 'what was it all about'? Was that all? Was it all because of the endless effort of our ancestors, the social democrats of yore? Because of a few years of life-existence? You could have saved a lot of trouble! The fun, walks, listening to music, writing poetry, going to the theater, riding, swimming, driving, dreaming, longing for childhood, having a family, playing games (this is what you will call work), these little pastimes, journeys and travel too — did *any* of this really make *any* sense? After all, there is no awareness and joy that remains from it. Everything just disappears. We are simply animals uniquely cast because we not only live, but also observe life and know something about life. We not only die, but we know in advance and can die whenever we wish. Suicide (the word murder would have long before been forgotten), free death, is actually what separates us from all other animals. Let's end the ridiculous comedy as quickly as possible because it leads to absolutely nothing. Let's kill each other. Let's do it but quickly, as soon as possible, in fact. This nonsense repeated over and over is so terribly boring! What do you say to that friend?

Shouldn't it be like that? — Do I hear an objection from you? You say it would never work that way. You deny socialism and think there is another way, something else perhaps? That is cowardice. I tell you that socialism is possible, without question and I will also tell you something else: that is a very high level of mankind. Or will you say the today's man is less inclined to think about death and free death? Perhaps this is true. But isn't this even more disgusting? And when one kills oneself once, not out of philosophy or boredom which is the same thing, but from necessity, out of common despair, is that not a vile and unworthy death? But if socialism can lead to nothing other than the philosophical mass death of humanity, and this is true, what other greater things do we have to preach than this death now in a million different tongues? — Wait, where are you going friend? Now that you've heard, do you wish to plunge into the world to preach death as my disciples? And don't you notice the contradiction that tickles me almost making me laugh? You are still too quick for me my companions young and old. You are not the first to let logic seduce you into all sorts of serious nonsense. I truly regret that logic has trapped you in the snares of my inconsistency. But I want to reveal to you what makes me laugh. How can one — preach death? Isn't wanting death the same as wanting to live? Isn't it possible to die without a word, eyes closed and without resignation? If other people are none of your business, why do you want to seduce them instead of leaving them alone? Please die friends, but die for yourselves. Die quiet and don't make a fuss! Am I not right?[7]

See what fools you are! You agree with me again. You've nearly brought me to tears. Why do you stand next to me if you haven't the same experiences? Your madness is completely different and simpler than mine. Look, I am not ready for death yet, far from it. I still have my joy of death. And this is why I speak my words to the whole human race, whoever wants to hear me or happens to hear me or didn't cover their ears quick enough. I enjoy people who do not yet know death and the longing for death. It gives me joy, superhuman joy to laugh at the crowd and to mock them and still bait them. I'm still alive because I enjoy

---

[7] It is worth considering the martyred spirit seeking the secrets of the earth. Landauer's own brutal murder and defiance at the end give this work, in particular, an autobiographical revelation. Ayn Rand in the dystopian novel "Anthem" describes a world of revealed secrets for those who seek them. In her work she describes lost the knowledge of "Unmentionable Times" and the "words of the Evil Ones" which are violently silenced by the authorities. When the members of "Equality 7-2521" witness a burning at the stake, they see in the eyes of the victim no pain or knowledge of the agony of the body. They see the eyes of the "Transgressor" selecting them alone from the crowd. "There was only joy in those eyes, and pride, a pride holier than is fit for human pride to be. And it seemed as if these eyes were begging us to gather that word and not let it go from us and from the earth."

playing with my pain and dragging my disgust out like a tough mead. I love death and that's why I live. I'm a superstitious person, why not? I shudder when I think about dying alone. It disgusts me to think what kind of stupid stuff people might suspect if I die alone and the nonsensical call me a suicide. I love the great death and I want companions which is why I preach death, because it allows a certain charm to life until the end. And you can trust that I will die, my friends. This is the only future I still acknowledge that coincides with my desires. It is all that I am going to die and want to die and what's more: I should die. The creeping death against the will on some straw sack is hateful to me. This death is a cancelled death which I laugh at. I will never die the death of vermin. Join me friends in the cry: Long live death!

Don't be alarmed at my horrible honesty. Or frightened. I am not honest for the sake of honesty. Truth is no longer a great leading word for me; I am only so because it gives me pleasure to play in a thousand colors and show you all my sides. I see through myself and laugh at myself when you see my backside and take my front seriously although you have seen the other side of my heart.

Moreover, I can say whatever I want. Those who understand me know my meaning in this writing. I renounce socialism because I don't like obtuse people and because I can no longer take life seriously. I preach death to those who take me and love me. With all my heart, I ask them to die with me and so to wait a little longer so we can all be together.

Those still groaning under the needs of life, the slaves of work, I advise them to hear me: do not be discouraged nor filled with hope either, but set yourselves free! Throw away the beggar's burden, not out of despair, rather from the understanding that life is a pointless thing. Then join me in my little band of death. If you are impatient and can't wait any longer then you won't die the beautiful death that I foolishly prepare for, but I wish you a good trip — and unconscious decay! The rest of you, I say goodbye at the great death. I wait for your echo and wish to speak with you again. But for socialism, I wish a long life and an old age and death on a mattress.

Karl Starkblom

PART 4

I promised to share the second letter on Karl Starkblom's preacher of death after a little while and share the replies to the first letter. Of course, I had thought differently and could be bitter now. My words found no answer, only an echo. I figured there were enough people to cheer me on with the words I spoke of redemption, but there was none of that. I thought my home would be filled with people every day, a crowd ready to talk things over with me. But no one came but a single person who shook my hand and then left. It was a worker. I received a few letters, some serious and others mocking. A few women and a couple of young single men declared themselves ready to die "if I was really serious." They all mentioned something like that.

My friends are not here so I can make a brief introduction. I am not living in the right time for me. I believed my writing could be understood as a literary event. Ridiculousness upon ridiculousness! Are you so unused to the printer's ink? Do you really think if a savior came today, he would stand on a mountain today and preach a sermon? And a train would blow past the embankment with its whistle? O, you imitators of everything that happened before. Of course, you would not understand my voice! I lacked the dignity and narrow-mindedness of the penitential preacher. You couldn't stand a laughing herald of new words yet. I'm sad. Very sad to be lonely in death as I was always in life.

Don't expect me to go into so-called criticism. Some would, but I don't wish to speak of them. They stand close, understand my speech — and yet, yet! They praise me like a chameleon or a writer who can do anything. Had they remained silent, come up to me to shake my hand, like the worker, then — yes! They lack reverence for me and themselves.

My friends who are not with me now! Sit in a circle and listen to me! When I rested in the forest, rode across the wet meadows and couldn't sleep — I dreamed the following below.

I wrote it all down and am going to have it printed too. Why am I doing this? To what purpose? O didn't you notice. Do you see the suffering that consumes me? I look for people! I look for people over and over again. I wish to speak to thousands of the them and to recognize them as my own and to seduce them to my death. And now I am looking for a simple person, only a person who loves me and wants to die with me. That's why I go into the Market Square and prostitute myself before all people, showing myself naked and clean.

Now hear the preacher of death's vision.

I want to tell you about a man who had no reason to laugh at himself. He believed in himself and found believers. Who was this lucky person? How was it possible for him? How do we imitate him? It was very easy for him, but not for us, even if we wanted to.

The man I am about to tell you about was epileptic. What, you exclaim in horror? How can you call this man happy? Yes, I call the man blessed that the illness of his spirit could break out in such a way. We are all epileptic. There is something in us that resists life, but woe to those whose illness is called spirit and whose medicine is the spirit! Far better are those whose bodies heal the mind and direct it towards the path of calm.[8] Some have only half of their brains because of the spasms and twitches that mix seriousness and groans like cries of pain in joy — that's just their bodies — as the soul knows nothing of spasms because it remains whole.

It is good for those who lose consciousness when they become insane! Heil the epileptic! They are prophets, saints and saviors. Look now here he comes! Doesn't he walk like a God? There he is in the midst of thousands in the assembly. Starkblom, the preacher of death, towers high above all the people! Can you

---

[8] translator: Some argue that the idea that the body can heal the mind is countered by Western medicine.

see him then! O be silent now. There is no need for admonition; everything listens breathlessly, being enticed sweetly by the magic of speech. O, how he has power over the hearts of men! How he subdues them and drives them to their knees in the dust. Honor death! Be faithful to death! Hold on! Soon you will die with me in greatness and freedom. Then the ugliness will stop. What was called human will disappear from the beauty of the goddess of nature. You will return home to the unconscious. You won't ask 'what for' anymore. The folly of the illusion of purpose has died with you. Nature is one, everything is beautiful, and nothing is perceived as one's own beauty. Time has dies with you. Cause and effect no longer live. A cheering of change will join with a pointless, senseless colorful and resounding coincidence. Die you individuals so that the madness of the whole may be dead. Die my brother, so that it may end. Laugh at the death of those who believe in the unconditional development in progress and the holy words. Die, die, shout death! The stream of people rolled by, bigger and bigger became the mass who were glad to die. — Where did the man go? Everything fled from my eyes. I hear no more. I feel my body as I lay on the floor. Where is Starkblom? Starkblom, where are you?

In every city there exists statues of princes and military leaders on pedestals in the marketplaces while the windows of the castles and palaces of the living are smashed into rubble. They have placed skeletons on the pedestals, idolized death, thrown off their clothes and danced around the images of death, cheering, laughing, and singing while music blares marching tunes. *Allons enfants, allons nousen!* Come children, let's go! The sun shines more golden than ever before as I fit wanted to warm people's lust for life in every pore and show them that man can live naked. But they want to die and Starkblom in terrible glory, dances the dance of death. In the evening, when it gets cooler and darker, the colors awaken in a fiery glow. They throw green, red and yellow cloths about themselves in a fantastic cast. There is inexpressble bliss and solemn whispers and music from the towers. Children jump from every corner doing summersaults and jumping over old people. They sit in a circle and listen to fairy tales about life. Distant winds blow through the streest and carry sweet scents with them from vast gardens and heaths outseide the city. Starkblom stands in the middle of the circle and raises his song oft he glorious future of this human world and how everything could be if we only wanted it. In the end, his words come back full of blissful happiness: "What a glory we fabricate —

what a beautiful world we destroy — we could win it for ourselves, but we die! — O!" Cheering, the crowd comes in and the wind rattles in the dead man's bones. The trumpets wring high in the air and the laughter of the crowd swells up like a roaring sea of trees that never ends. A proud tall woman steps up to Starkblom in middle of the scene, O!

The lamps extinguish and there is a shrill fanfare in the middle of everything. An infinite cloth spreads over everything – night, night — void, void – where is the woman? Where are the people? Where is death? Starkblom sits on the sofa and leans his head into his hands — everything is different, so different. Everything seems dull and ordinary, low and mediocre. O where are you greatness of thought and appearance? I want to fall asleep and not dream anymore — O to cry or laugh, no more of these chocking sobs, this place between crying and laughing; Everything about me twitches, but I can't dance. I groan, O if I could sing! I can't take this anymore, I will die soon, soon! o ugh, ugh! What is life but missing surprise, and chance, just suddenness and blindness? Where there is tradition, mediation and reckoning? The taking account of what has been, and what is to come? O, nature how I envy your happiness! You see this waterfall beginning high in the mountain all the way to the depths. How the waves wander so peacefully, how glad she is for her green banks, flowers, and stones sprung up — an occurrence never suspected. She falls deep down, O this roaring and foaming and jubilation of never returning! The bliss of forgetting, rediscovery and then forgetting again. How many waves have fallen, perfectly unknown, nothing binding the individual drops that separate each other in their glory? But with us — we are eternal! Don't we wish to kill finally the past? Aren't we decrepit yet? I am, I am — breaking down under the weight of the past. Oh, I could kill all tradition, then I'd want to live. I could kill the past if I killed myself. Then, I'd be part of nature — no, no then I no longer exist. It is nature then. I hate you fools because you want to live! I don't want to die yet. I must wait to see if you decide to come with me and thereby extinguish the human. O, I wouldn't talk with you if I only knew how to extinguish you! All of you! I don't wish for someone to come along after my death and experience this same thing. I don't wish it. I want my death to have meaning. I am disgusted at my last thought. I feel disgusted at being all alone.

The great event that Starkblom has always proclaimed has occurred. The entire civilized world has been conquered by a sect of "degenerate old crazy bon vivants", as radical party leaders put it. All who came in contact with the movement were carried away by a religious frenzy. The great mass of workers who had previously followed socialism have grown tired in life. They realized that the negative revolutionary subversive passion has reason as its justification, but no purpose. They realized no purpose e.g., the delusion that creates justice, but in this case a result which is oppression and hopelessness. They want to perish. Well, this they have done already. But they wanted first to tear it all down! Is it vengeance that drives it? Madness? Seduction? Who knows and what does it matter? One no longer thinks in this time of shocking dissolution rather one enjoys one's passion and undertakings. They stop working and smash the machine s. Armies are infected and plow the ocean. Men and women stop wearing clothing and walk naked through the streets as they no longer fear illness knowing it will be their last. State power is powerless and ceases altogether. One steals his requirements; the supply is large enough for a short time. Amidst the terrible ferocity of club and fang everywhere, most are flooded with an inkling of blissful beauty of their unconscious existence; men and women embrace in public places; murders occur whenever someone comes into another's place, countless couples are dying and almost all the newborns are put to death.

Things degraded to the point where Starkblom had a violent crying fit and the next day suffered from an epileptic attack from which he didn't want to awaken. When he recovered after a few days, he again led the movement, as far as he could. He didn't want to be deceived by the apparent victory of his cause because there was still much to be done. Most of the time, he sat around in a quiet room surrounded by confidants making plans or holding councils of war.   Perhaps at some future time, civilized people could develop again from wild peoples that remained unspoilt. That couldn't be. He suggested equipping a huge campaign into the interior of Africa. But one of his disciples said that this had already been going on for some time. Perhaps one should send preachers there. The idea of death is so simple and convincing that even uncivilized persons understand it. In the meantime, one must begin preaching in Europe about the great death.   Otherwise the movement will flatten out again. Now is the time for action.

But what about the highly developed animals, objected another. They have self-awareness, make no mistake about it. Wouldn't it be disgusting if we died

and had to let them live. Dogs, horses, ants, bees —
these should be exterminated root and branch.

O, we do everything do piecemeal, sighed a very
young man who had been amongst the most
passionate about the movement. I'm afraid thinking
organisms also live on Mars. We can't reach them
either. We want to die right now, but we can't always
do everything we want. We should be able to destroy
not just people, animals, the earth but all of nature
and the whole world. And can we do that?

The others shouted: Accursed traitor! Unfaithful!
You denigrate our worthy cause. They came at him
with raised fists and swords drawn.

The young man laughed wildly. Ha, haha! You friends
of death wish to kill me? Leave me to live, that would
be the right punishment! But you fools warned me
rightly. When I am dead, so is the world — to me.
What do I care about you all? He went into the next
room where a beautiful girl slept, completely
exhausted from the wild rage of the days. He woke
her and held her firmly. Then he tore open the
window and held her tightly in his arms while leaning
forward. On big push and the people below would
find two shapeless bodies. Starkblom experienced it
before his eyes. He was having the familiar feeling of
another attack. It passed, then he gave a short laugh.

The man was right. Our time is coming soon. Let the others then look after themselves.

Do you dread me and my Doppelgänger? You turn away in horror at the effusions from my crazed brain. I tell you, I praise this Starkblom. He's got real happiness, even before death. He believes in himself. Like the cherry tree that blossoms before the frost comes, or the avalanche that crashes down into the valley. Didn't you know that nature is cruel to the weak spectator? Why then are you staying outside, you little fools, with your thinking and woe, and morals and your pants? — Part of Starkblom is once again happy and in good spirits today. The other half suspects death, recklessness and self-evidence, the roll of the dice and coolness which fools call boldness. I don't give a damn about you. At least you can live because of me. O, you amuse me! It shouldn't occur to yuou to despair and whine and desire death or think you would be like me! Who knows — if I want to continue living — to enjoy my laughter for awhile longer?

And the armies of the dying swelled and became stronger and stronger. Suddenly the battle was over. Isolated shots ceased to rattle in all the corners of Europe and entire cities blew themselves up. Rural people streamed in from all sides, as if on command,

and threw themselves into the flames of the burning streets and forests. Railway trains drove in all directions towards to seas and soon not only thousands and hundreds of thousands but millions and millions of people were sunk into the depths of the oceans. Often the house pets were taken along, but nothing else. Starkblom stayed in the center of Germany along with a few loyal people and directed the movement. He sent people out and soon they would return like the doves with olive branches: there were no more people to be seen. Suddenly he left his surroundings and travelled away. He went missing. His followers fell into feverish excitement. One was already mumbling something about the traitor. He wanted to drive them all top their deaths and live all alone. But that would be incorrect — initially. He wanted to see the pure earth once more. And he saw his fill. — Never in his life had he felt so blessed and exalted as when he wandered all alone through the valleys and mountains, saw ruins of cities and villages and shouted into the air. Alone! Alone in nature! Then a mad thought took hold of him. One night he approached the place again and crept into their camp where his followers lived. He seemed to have succeeded without being seen. He found the tent of the woman he was looking for and woke her. He whispered excitedly to her and held her in his arms.

She shook all over. He seemed to be winning her — she followed him. They fled out into the solitude of a wondrous valley. Nobody knew where they had gone. Adam and Eve! He exulted when they were finally alone. It seemed they had been saved. We two, alone in paradise! They may die, so let them die! We can stay behind and start a new race. We want to live, create a new wonderful life and be one with nature and reason. — In the meantime, their escape had been discovered and something bad was suspected. A search commenced. After a few weeks, however, he volunteered to join his band of friends — alone. "Forgive me my friends," he said amiably but to the point. "I made a last attempt. But it was impossible. That's the least of it. I strangled the woman with these hands. Well, let's die now. I am ready to go."

They moved to the sunny banks of the Rhine. It was the time of the wine blossoms. Many wondrous comedies played on as if all were reluctant to part with the thought of death. Because they suspected that once they were dead, they would get little pleasure from it. Starkblom warmed up and became extremely talkative again. "What would the earth do without us?" He said once. We seemed to be its greatest entertainment. I for one hope she's bored to death without us and plunges straight into the sun. Maybe that will mix it all up and then everything will become one again. Nothing would be separate anymore. You know, I want to say: one and nothing — it's all the *same*. It was the particularity and difference that created the world and life consciousness. Once the world becomes one again, there is nothing to behold, absolutely nothing. Then they threw themselves into the waters — all of them. After a time, the laughter and singing and fearful screams ceased — then a few screamed and the total earth was without a human. The Rhein flowed on calmly. Soon the animals of the forest pricked up their ears and drank cool waters. Green vegetation grew over the whole earth and took over human dwellings. Birds sang and there was jubilation like never before. The flowers bloomed and smelled in never before sweet splendor. The trees rustled and spoke to the winds. Storms howled and the earth roared along its path. He was dead! He was dead! The great tormentor of the earth was dead!

And now, I grab my head and hope the reader does the same. Calm yourself down, nobody is getting murdered. I'm not going to kill off Starkblom, the preacher of death, the epileptic, just the original Starkblom, the Starkblom the sufferer and Starkblom the dying. It's true I am going to die and you shan't hear from me anymore. For the last time I wish you a warm farewell from this world.

Part Five

A few weeks after Starkblom's pamphlet appeared, a young woman was bent over a table in a bright attic apartment in Paris. She was busy packing essentials into a small travel bag. A man with a close-cropped beard who appeared much younger than his gray hair and lined face lay in the sofa. He was smoking a cigarette and smiling like a rascal who had succeeded in some fine plan. He admired the wonderful figure of the woman. She had a very common shape. She was nothing less than slim with a broad face which showed uncommon benevolence. Her large eyes seemed kind and understanding of the world; her forehead was free; neither high nor arched. Her hair was cut short and parted straight. She finished and closed the bag. "Say Hansa," she resumed the conversation. "Don't you really want to come along straight away?" "I would like to go too, but it's the strangest thing in my entire life. Which is pretty strange." He laughed. "No, my dear Marguerite, I won't be coming along. It would be in my plans at all.

You understand what I mean, yes? Of course, you must not mention me. You have to pretend I don't exist. When you think it's time, telegraph me. I'll come immediately. I am so happy and think it will work. "

"I just don't know. I am not comfortable with it. For example, if he shows me the door as soon as I have entered his room." "He certainly wouldn't do that. The man is miserably lonely that's obvious from every line." I suspect something completely different. He smiled and whistled to himself. "Well?" "Hm, hm."

"I don't know. It's possible he's killed himself before I get there." "Hm. Of course, it's not impossible. Such things can't be discounted. Dying is mostly a matter of a moment. But I don't believe that with him. You know I share a similar feeling with him. We are men in waiting. He thinks about it a hundred times and suddenly on an impulse he doesn't carry it out. Do you know what I mean?"

He looked at her in the face.

"He's going to fall in love with you Marguerite. It will be a great, passionate love."

She blushed, but did not look away.

"And I?"

"That I cannot say. I don't know him. But I don't think it's impossible that you too — well, we shall see.

You know in such a case you don't need to consider me. "Yes, I know. The same goes for me my dear Hansa."

"Well, that's why we've been together so long," he said with shining eyes. He pressed her hand to his lips.

Then he jumped up and paced the room. He stopped in front of Marguerite again. "I am delighted about this, really. I am royally pleased by this situation. Whenever I start to get bored, fate sends me something new and better. You know, these bombshells are getting really boring."

"But these are capable, unusual people. You know this certainly. But I liked them better in the beginning. Now that there are consequences, arrests have been made and others are being deported, they are gaining a pathos. Some have already become martyrs. And you know that doesn't bode well for them."

"Jean, you're exaggerating. What you call pathos is merely mockery. I think they are free people who consider themselves nothing really special. But they find the world much less so." Well, I am happy to give you pleasure. But in the long run it's not for me. Still there is something serious about it and you know I don't like that. It's good that the story got in the way."

"You have a right to be serious about it. I mean very seriously."

"You think so? I don't deny it. Only because I enjoy it."

Well, that's a kind of explanation, like any other. My white Pythia, I already know you are a bit different from me. So now, I am sending you to see a terribly serious guy. I don't fear him. I also think he's come close to our point of view. He's just a nudge away. Do you know what is mainly missing in him?"

"Now? By the way it is soon time for you. He lacks nature. He has understanding. Nature ...

"Nature?" "I am missing that too." "Only you have it my Maguerite. "But I've made a replacement of it in my life. It is something great that man can now create his own comfortable existence, far away from nature. Unlike her." "Well, we are all shipwrecked. You just don't think about it anymore. But now I have to go." She put on her hat.

"So, goodbye my darling, live well — I'll accompany you to the train. So, you understand everything. You will do well."

"I understand everything. I don't do it for your sake, but because I need to see the man and help him. I'll do what I can."

"Good, very good." Come and let me kiss you before we go."

Marguerite leaned down and kissed him. Then the unlikely couple went down the stairs.

Two days later, around 9AM, Marguerite stood in front of the white house. She looked at the villa for a while and took a breath. Then she opened the front door and climbed the stairs. See didn't see anyone in the hallway. She knocked on the door, but there was no answer. She opened it. It was a bedroom that had recently been vacated. The bed was unmade and the air in the room was stale. She paused a moment between the doors and quickly entered in a determined way. The closed door led to another room. She heard footsteps and some confused humming. That had to be him. She put the travel bag on the table and took off her hat. She poured some water over her hands and wet her eyes and hair. After she dried herself, she stood for a while. She rested her hands on her chest. Her breath was heavy. Then she knocked on the connecting door. She dropped her hand and shook her head. "This isn't going anywhere," she whispered softly. She boldly opened the door and stopped, holding her breath. At the opposite window a man in shirtsleeves stood with his back to her. His eyes looked down on the valley. His hands strained to put on a collar which was probably too tight for him. Again, she heard the little groan. The corner of her mouth twitched slightly. Suddenly his hand released the collar and he stamped his foot violently and hit his forehead with his fist. He shouted out loud, "Good heavens, I am being driven mad!"

Marguerite couldn't bare it anymore. She laughed. Starkblom winced and turned around quickly. "How, what ... who are you? What do you want? How did you get here?" "Later. Perhaps you will allow me to help you close your collar first?"

Starkblom looked mistrustfully at her.

"Excuse me, but how did you get in here? Where is your hat?"

"I left it in the next room. I didn't see anyone and walked in. I've travelled a long way to have a word with you. Now allow —"

Starkblom's expression brightened. He laughed. "So, you've read —? The pamphlets? Is it not?   And you came to me. Nice. And now you wish to fit my collar? Well, it's all my fault. She stepped closer and began working. "My you are large! Please keep still Monsiuer otherwise it won't work." "Be careful, please, you're strangling me!"

She dropped her hand again and looked him in the face and laughed. "Was that so terrible?" "Well yes, just laugh at me. Is that why you came here?" "Well, partly."

"Aha. Well then, I would ask you to put my collar in order and then, yes then you will probably be able to run along. Or was there something else that would find amusing?" "Certainly, certainly, something else too. But rest now. So, we're done here. Is it too tight?" Starkblom gave her a look. "No", he said quickly. He walked around the room a little longer then took his shirt from the hook on the wall and put it on. "So, would you like to sit down, Fräulein? Or, " It doesn't matter. But call me Mrs." She sat down at the table.

Starkblom remained standing before her and watched. He scratched his forehead. He found the situation rather uncomfortable. "Where are you from?" "Paris." "Ah, a beautiful city".

"Oh, yes."

"I was never there. Strange."

There was a pause. Then Starkblom began again: "Well if you've read that thing and understood, then you know me a little." "I don't feel like talking." "Me neither." "My throat is tight –"Marguerite smiled good-naturedly. "Hell, I'm thinking of that bloody collar again. Oh, women, women!" Do you know about women? Starkblom gave her a long look.

"Really, not particularly. I had a wife once, when I was still — this doesn't interest you. What is it you want?"

"I am interested, Starkblom. Back when you were still – happy?"

"Ah, happiness. I was a philistine. She was something of a woman. She is fortunate to be gone now. She wouldn't understand me today. Nobody does. Cursed world." "I think I understand and that is why I've come. Do you want to listen to me? I read both letters, both. I've looked into the deep abyss of your thoughts and gloom. You were looking for someone and I came to you. You are looking for someone who be with you —" Starkblom had stopped listening. He walked impatiently back and forth with small steps then opened the door and listened outside a few steps from Marguerite.

"Would you like to eat breakfast with me? I'm hungry."

"I think you are mocking me now," replied Marguerite, blushing.

"What? Did I miss something? Do you think I can live on air?" Or, oh well – yes, I wasn't listening to you. You can give your beautiful speech later. Finally, where have you been all this time?" — This last thing he said to the housekeeper who came in the tea, cold roast meat and wine. She opened he eyes wide when she saw such an unfamiliar visitor. "You can ask questions later, another cup and plate, quickly!"

Then he turned to the strange woman. "You must have an appetite. Please take some." And so, he did. He pushed his plate and mug over to Marguerite. "I can't wait". You are very kind, Mr. Starkblom. Let's have breakfast together. Do you always drink wine this early?" "Yes, I've gotten used to it lately. Well, now we can begin." The housekeeper had brought the essentials. Marguerite first poured tea, then wine for himself. Starkblom glanced over at her a few times during dinner. Finally, he spoke while chewing: what kind of healthy teeth you have, and this hunger! And the whole figure, where does such a person come from. You don't seem German based on your accent." Marguerite laughed.

"Well, where to begin. I was born in Alsace, but came to France quite early." Starkblom was still looking at her. "Splendid, splendid," he muttered. Marguerite blushed.

He raised his glass.

"Well, a toast, my lady — what was your name? May I know?"

She clinked glasses with him.

"And what do we let live?" She asked alluding a smile.

"Life ... life? Oh, do you remember what you wanted?" He looked at her deeply in her eyes.

"Death —? With —?" She lowered her eyes and scratched the plate with the knife. "Maybe," she said softly.

"Well cheers," he broke off suddenly, then he drained the glass with one gulp.

Shortly afterwards he got up and went to the window. "Have you had enough already."

"Yes, I'm not feeling well." Marguerite laid down her knife and fork. She stared straight ahead.

Suddenly she was overwhelmed by the awareness of what she had done and the entire situation. She put her hands over her face. She stayed like that for some time. Suddenly Starkblom stood at the window and said in a very sad tone without looking back: "Well,

Mrs. Marguerite, do you want to give your speech now? What are you prepared for? What do you think of me?" Marguerite dropped her hands; she was blushing red. Then she got up, but stopped at the table and said timidly: "Let me leave, I don't know — it's wrong, it's not working —."

Starkblom turned to her and looked at her with amazement. He thought he had an idea about what was going on inside her. He remained silent for a long time and just looked at her. Then he spoke: "Perhaps the feeling you had was right when you came. Don't be afraid." He took her hand. "If you don't feel like speaking now, just stay. We have time. Or did you have a special reason or some event in the last part of your life that gives you cause to visit me?"

"No, that's not it." "But have you misjudged me? Do you despise me?"

Starkblom became embarrassed and he knew not what to say. Finally, he stuttered, "I beg you ... but Mrs. Marguerite ... but please disregard ... whatever are you thinking about? You seem to me one ... exquisite woman. I understand you, but am not sure how you got here. Don't you want to tell me something — about your life?

Marguerite sat down on the sofa again and slowly ran both hands over her dark dress. He stood in front of her and crossed his legs while leaning on the table looking at her all the while.

"Well, there isn't much to tell. I am the child of well-off farmers. Then I went to a monetary in France to be educated as a child. There I ran away – with, well it doesn't matter. It happened a long time ago. There I came to a society of free people, men and women, mainly Russians and Poles. Since then I've read and done a lot. Well, I just became free through all that."

"Hmm, wonderful, very much so. What did you mean by "become free"?

"Well I mean you should know that too. I have few prejudices, and understand many people including people of different kinds. I can find my way into many things and for the rest, follow my nature as it is.   It has been through things in the past, different circumstances. Above all I call that free. That a person is not ashamed of doing a thousand of things a day that the mind cannot explain or approve of. For example, to live and be happy without having to give a reason for it."

"Are you a philistine without prejudice?"

"Yes, yes," she answered briskly. "I accept that. You have to be a philistine, but an ideal one. You can't live without that, —" she added with certainty.

"And I say: one will not," cried Starkblom and slapped the table. Well, die then. I mean you shouldn't want to. Well that's it. It is a theory. I can believe that; I completely understand. As it stands today, we cannot understand what we are living for. That's all very good. I admit that. We have nothing positive to acknowledge, absolutely nothing. And we will never go back to the old positions ever. We'd be ashamed. We are not Romantics, nor Philistines in the old sense. But we wait and that's reason enough for us to live. We are curious."

"What then are we waiting for?"

"Now I don't know. Something false or wrong, probably. But necessary. Something that needs something new that is overwhelming, a new, enduring superstition, a new religion, even if it is no longer clothed in those words. Simply something positive that makes sense to everyone. Something that has meaning for everyone. It overwhelms everyone. We all have an inkling that something is in the air. It is something big, and unheard of. They wanted to create it too. But they could only destroy, not create. Let us wait, and if we live, let us live joyfully. Let us enjoy our pain too. It's part of it for sure. But none of this is new to you. They just didn't have words for it. Maybe they were ashamed. But we really needn't be ashamed of that. We are transitional people and we feel as much. And those that have been through as much as you, those aren't just words. There has never been a time like ours. And the time to come — might it be even more unheard of — more powerful? Am I not right?" Starkblom had listened to her with admiration.

He would not have believed such a woman lived. Now she was sitting there on the sofa and looked at him kindly with shimmering eyes. It seemed like a fairy tale to him. He answered with a mechanical search for a familiar thought.

"I don't know if you are right. I find such a life disgusting too. And the time to come; what does that matter? It's about us, about me."

"Yes, of course, but just because of that. But our thoughts and dreams about the future and above all, our curiosity, how much of it we experience ourselves and how our perspectives change — this is only a part of us. You say: we are no longer interested in anything. Well, I say we are still interested in many things. You disagree: you say we shouldn't care. This is not true. You tyrannize yourself with you constant brooding. Man is not just a mind. When you say: I will not love, this is only a part of you. There is another part that says oh yes, he wants to live and should not endure subjugation. This part is stronger than all the rest. It should be. Your mind is draining you. But the other is still alive in you. I can feel it, and it shows in your writings. This is a good thing. In any other case the matter would be desperate. Only you can only save yourself. This is why I came to see you, to tell you this. Return to life! — Life is beautiful —."

Starkblom looked down for a long while. Then he spoke softly: "I know everything you are saying. You guessed right; nothing is new to me. Such has tried to rise up in me many times; especially of late, but I fought it. The spirit is the highest thing man possesses. Only a coward suppresses it. You propose that other instincts rule over those of the spirit. I can no longer agree with this; perhaps I could earlier. That would be too horrid for me now — in the long view of things."

"O, no, this isn't so at all. I argue for enjoyment, yes, but also spiritual joy especially. This kind of enjoyment, spiritual, is only possible in connection with others. We say: instincts. Otherwise it degenerates and leads to destruction. You want to deny it, but you cannot. Do you not find pleasure in such conversation? Where you don't have to force yourself into asking out of habit and persistence: what is the purpose of this? Asking what's behind it?"

Starkblom became restless; he couldn't bear her eye which she turned full and calm onto him. He rose and looked out of the window. But she persisted. She felt she had struck a chord in him. She was glad her mind could lock onto his in conversation.

"Tell me again, Starkblom", she began again, "about the woman in your last pamphlet. At two places." "That was rather sudden. What did you want with that?"

"It might be symbolic. I confess I did not understand it."

Starkblom turned around quickly. "I shouldn't be symbolic." Then he added hesitating. "It was probably an urge. Half longing, half suspicion — it was nonsense, nonsense."

"Perhaps I understand now," she said softly. "That too is part of it. You can be saved, certainly."

Now he looked her straight in the eye. "Marguerite, Marguerite," he cried. "You are playing a dangerous game. I am still alive, you see, I am still human!

Beware!" He held out his hand as if he were searching for her. "I am glad you are alive", she smiled somewhat fearfully and bending back a bit," but you are a child." He ran his hand over his forehead in confusion. "How ... what?" "You mean ... but no, not that, not that. No. No. I do not want this. Die with me Marguerite, I beg you, die with me. I don't want to live anymore. I cannot."

Marguerite stood up, breathing heavily and very pale. "Starkblom", she said, "you should not be stubborn. You are harming yourself. I might do it if –"

She stopped. Starkblom took her hand and looked at her feverish eyes. "What would you do? What? Marguerite?!" She could only whisper. "Die, of course, what else?" Starkblom also took her other hand. "Would you do it, Marguerite? You would? Yes?" Marguerite could no longer speak. She sank into the armchair, leaned back and let her head sink to the side. "Yes, yes, yes. If you want. But not now, not now. We will wait. There are concerns. O, it cannot be."

Starkblom stepped back, as if suddenly disillusioned. "Yes, we want to wait. Maybe – oh, nonsense." Then he grabbed his head as if exhausted by excitement. "What a day this has been! Who would have guessed? Who would have guessed?" Suddenly the corners of his mouth twitched. His eyes lit up madly. Then a fine almost malicious smile crept across of face. "I think we are lying to each other Marguerite. No?" And in a whisper he uttered: "we aren't speaking of the same thing — no? "

Marguerite beckoned weakly with both hands to stop.

"Let it alone, Starkblom. I want to die with you — or live as you wish. But please be quiet now, I ask you."

"I cannot anymore."

She leaned back wearily and closed her eyes.

Starkblom went to the window and stared out. Then he looked at her for a long time. A trembling overcame him. He turned away again, forcing himself to look at the trees opposite and up at the clouds. He remained like that for a long time.

At last Marguerite ran her hand lightly over her forehead as if she were chasing away a dream. Then she clenched a fist and ran her hand up and down her arm. She gained control over herself again. She let her eyes wander around the room. Books and magazines lay jumbled up on the table. They under a thick blanket of dust. She stepped closer and thoughtlessly painted characters and letters on the volumes. She picked up one of the books and looked at the title. "Ah," she said happily. "What have we here? „'Also sprach Zarathustra' by Friedrich Nietzsche. I've never picked it up, but have heard alot about it. I'd like to learn about it."

"You don't know it? Well, good for you. You won't be able to learn much from him anymore. But the language! The *language*. It's a wonderful book. Let me see it. I'll show you something." He took the book from her hand, sat down, opened it to a random place and began to read. He read one section after another and continued. She gradually calmed down. They then continued to speak for a long time deeply and on different things. Later they went for a walk and sat in the countryside. Marguerite talked about her youth, and various people she met. She had a lot to explain and talked freely. She was; however, silent about the last years of her life. In the evenings, they said goodnight to each other rather early and cautiously, almost ceremoniously. Marguerite went to the guest room which had never been used since Starkblom lived there. She looked out of the window a little longer and let the night air cool her down. Then she lay down in bed, crossing her hands under her head as was her custom when she wanted to think. Throughout the day, from time to time, she had to think of something. She didn't want to forget it and now she reflected. But before she got that far, her thoughts fluttered into confused dreams and she fell asleep. Starkblom sat on his bed and brooded for a long while. Should he be as happy and playful as a great child or should he hate himself? He really didn't know. He had his knees up and propped his elbow on them, holding his head. He starred with narrow eyes and pressed lips. It never occurred to him to be surprised that his fate as it was being fulfilled, was the most natural story in the world. Suddenly it no longer held him as something pressed against the rigid wall of his mouth and he burst out loud and laughed while clapping his thigh with the flat of his hand. He laughed at himself with a youthful joy. And because he sensed it, he had to laugh even more. What a fool! What a fool!

He quickly undressed and turned off the bedroom light. He tossed and turned a few times, then he closed his eyes and lay still. "So now we must fall asleep, understand?' But Starkblom didn't want to understand. He laughed a little again. Then he opened his eyes and stared at the ceiling for a long time. And as if something were pulling him up, he straightened his upper body, waved his hand in the air and said in an audible voice, "Good night, Marguerite! — Good night, dear Marguerite!" He lay down quietly again and smiled tiredly. The dreams that came were excited and followed each other in a confused order, some with eyes opened, other with closed eyes. So, he passed most of the night tossing and turning without sleepiness.   It was as if he had lost the haze of fog in which he otherwise rested well and slept deeply.   His head was incredibly clear. His eyes were cool and would not stay closed despite the dreadful dreams. It was quite natural that he could not sleep because he had no reason to sleep. It wasn't until late morning that he cleaned up a little.

For the next few days, they lived quietly and idyllically side by side. They read, chatted and went for walks in the country. Otherwise they held back shyly and no longer wanted to think of the other. It occurred to Marguerite that she shouldn't forget, but she didn't want to think about it. It will be found, she thought over and over. She wanted to let go.

Starkblom; however, let himself be carried away as if by a storm. He couldn't return. He couldn't hold on anymore. It had come over him. He had to go forward with it. Just go into the flood! Who knows? Yes!

One evening as they were about to part before sleep, Starkblom put his trembling hand on her shoulder. His knees trembled.   His face was pale and his eyes burned. He tried to say in a calm tone: "Marguerite, we must come to some conclusions: why not?"

She looked at him with horrified eyes: "You want to die? Now?" He cried out loudly: "Don't lie, Marguerite, don't lie! To die?! Who is thinking about death? I want to live! You! You!" His voice broke. Then he added more calmly, almost solemnly. "Marguerite, I am the man!" She looked at him seriously and crossed her arms over her chest. She spoke painfully: "I am the woman, yes!" She nodded affirmatively and then bowed her head and didn't look up.

He bit his lip and let out a long breath while staring into the air. He stepped back and looked up at her. Suddenly he grabbed her by the shoulders and pulled her close. She let it happen. The he whispered, trembling, "Thank you. Please come over."

He lay with her and comforted her. He embraced her and all the shame and disgust that had threatened to overwhelm him vanished. As he lay dull and motionless, the leaden languor of his soul broke away from him and strength, joy and blissful abeyance made their victorious entrance. He never tired of looking into Marguerite's calm, sweet, comforting eye. He did do calmly and without excitement as he kissed her face and mouth. Again, and again his soul and body rose to this quiet woman who sometimes stroked his hair and wiped the sweat from his forehead. Sometimes the spoke together during the long, beautiful night. The sounds drifted away in the dark like a golden dream caressing the plumage of the night birds, their soft tones and gentle whirring falling silent again.

When morning's misty fingers wiped the dark from the windows the two separated in tiredness delivering them both into a deep, dreamless sleep.

In the late morning Starkblom suddenly sat up startled and looked around in confusion. He realized what had happened and saw his sleeping companion. He lay back down and smiled. Fresh and alter, he could fall back to sleep. He looked at Marguerite and her chest rising and falling evenly. Her cheeks were pink like he'd never seen. He stayed like that for a long time, not wanting the take his eyes off of her. He would have liked to sleep again. He laid his head on her chest as gently as he could and turned his body to see her face. Soon Marguerite's mouth twitched, perhaps frightened by a disturbing dream. She moaned softly then woke and looked into Starkblom's eyes. Neither spoke a word and an unspeakable serenity transfigured her features; they kept looking at each other. Suddenly, Marguerite bent down, put her arms around his neck and kissed him deeply.

"Good morning dear," she said cheerfully. "Good morning, Marguerite," replied Starkblom happy and grateful. While the two lay quietly together, he began, "Something just came to me now which I hadn't thought about."

"What then?"

"That was the first kiss you ever gave me."

"So?" She blushed. "Yes, and?"

"You know, I don't like to use old words. They become so worn and base. But you understand me as I meant it ... so ... well —."

"Is it really so horrible, Karl? What do you mean?"

"I mean, now that you've kissed me, and before that — I mean to say, do you love me Marguerite?"

Then Marguerite pressed he hands over her eyes, frowned and nodded her head slowly and solemnly several times as children do to confirm something in a serious way. Then she laughed to herself and whispered in his ear. "Yes." Starkblom took her hand and squeezed it tightly and never let it go. He lay back down on his back and dreamt. He smiled until his eyes filled with tears. "What's happening?" Asked Marguerite.

"Oh, I just remembered something," he said, smiling. "What, tell me."

He was silent, then he said:" "My poor little Lorchen." "Your wife?" She said softly. He nodded. She was filled with shame and never knew why. Something serious floated through the room. Full of the dark feelings, she leaned over to him and kissed his forehead. After a while he asked her, "Have you ever had a child, Marguerite?

"No," she said blushing a little.

Then he got up and knelt in front of her. He placed his hands on her head. "You will have one." She covered her face with her hands then lay there nodding thoughtfully.

She got up quickly and they both dressed. "Do you know what I think of my last pamphlet now?" "No, what?" "Listen. Man in his forties, widower, looking for partner in an unusual way. Must be tall and sturdy, very educated and free from prejudice. Please send offers using the following code: Long live death! Wasn't that it?"

"And the strangest thing is that I found the beautiful thing. How did you come about, Marguerite? How did you get my ads in Paris?"

Marguerite had laughed at first, but now she turned serious and a little pale. "It wasn't so easy dear. It had to do with something different. But now I can't possibly tell you. You have to wait. Soon – OK?"

"As you wish Marguerite. I have you and we have each other, and that's all that matters. Everything else doesn't matter." They spend the following day in a blissful and all-forgetting mood. What could have disturbed such happiness?

Sometimes Starkblom became overwhelmed and the past sought to grab him again with its murderous paws. It's at those times he said "My happiness is too great. I shall die soon." It wasn't too difficult for the two to scare away the ghosts. One afternoon they sat cheerfully on the balcony, chatting and looking down into the green valley. The housekeeper, with raised eyebrows and an amazed look brought a telegram. She handed it to Starkblom with some doubtful look.

He took it quickly and read the address. His face held a puzzled look. He motioned for the woman to go.

"Is it for you Marguerite?" He handed her the dispatch. She read the address and blushed all over.

It said, "Mrs. Marguerite Starkblom. Villa White House." "Yes." She whispered. The paper remained in her lap.

"That's strange," said Starkblom, staring at her. "Do you understand? Can't you tell me? Who knows about this? Who reported it —?"

"It's different dear Karl. Just be patient. Let me read it first. Maybe then-." She broke the seal and read a few words. "Why do I hear nothing from you? I was expelled from France and am on my way. Arriving today. Hopefully all is well. Jean."

She handed the paper without emotion. He read it and looked at her questioningly and sadly. "Marguerite, what does this mean? Who is this man? How does he know you-? Did you write to him from here?"

"No."

"But how does he know then? What's this? Marguerite!" She whispered, "I lived with him. I came here with his consent. He is – "She fell silent. "With his consent? I don't understand. Marguerite! What's this? How can he call you Starkblom?"

"He calls himself that, Karl and I named myself after him. Oh, it doesn't matter."

"Doesn't matter, really? And his name is Starkblom.
Wouldn't that be an unheard-of coincidence? Is this
a dream? "

"It's no coincidence -or -the way you might think it.
His name is Johannes Starkblom. He thinks he's your
brother." Starkblom realized. He got up quickly.
"What, Johannes? He's alive? And you — with him
— oh, Marguerite what kind of story is this?" He sat
back down on the chair. He was exhausted. This
situation got to him. "I don't care about my siblings.
Not at all. But that — that's something else. But you-
!" Marguerite held him close and put her arm around
his neck. You are so close my dear. See, I can't help it
and neither can he. But he predicted it. " "What did
he say?" "Here's how it came about. We agreed not
to see one another anymore. He didn't mean it like
that. He's really a great person. I am still quite fond
of him."

"So, Marguerite, what about me?"

"But my dear Karl, that's quite different — it can't go
on – you know – I'm in love with you Karl! Do you
understand?"

"My dear Marguerite, I believe you. I'm not a
Philistine! Just that it's my brother-!"

"But if it wasn't for that, I would never have come to you." "No?" "Will you listen now?" "This is also true."

"Yes, tell me then, I am calmer now. It's a person. Johannes! He's still alive!"

"Of course, he lives! He's been in Paris for years. I met him two years ago and we've been living together for about a year. He's been through an awful lot in life. He's not introverted like you. But he's been around. He's been shaken. Well, because of those experiences he became completely free. More than any of us. He's practical. Never paid much attention to theory. He goes along with everything that excites the nerves, what's new. That's what amuses him. And he's such a kind hearted person. But you can't tell him that. He doesn't see it that way."

"I see him now. The good-for-nothing! I had no idea that would become of him. He always did the opposite of what I did. And now we're almost in the same place. Yes, yes, the world is round! He's being expelled now? Why?" "Because of his activities with the anarchists. We participated in a few things." Starkblom got up and paced back and forth. "O' the lucky one! You are the lucky ones! What did I do to get where I am now! All the thinking and brooding; it almost broke me! Everything inside pressed me to go crazy. And you – and him! He does this and that! He thinks he's carefree!

"And he's not epileptic," said Maria smiling. "He doesn't have what I have. I am so clumsy. I have so many old things that I need to unburden myself from. And now I am too old! What would I be if I didn't have you? And now he's taking you away from me? Marguerite! Don't leave me! I ... you ... I need you! Marguerite hugged him tighter. "My dear Karl, he cannot part us. He doesn't wish to. We will always be together. And finally —. She stopped. Then she added. "You'll see. We'll wait for him. Does that cheer you up a bit?"

"I don't know. Perhaps. I'm afraid. —How did you get my writings?"

"Oh, he reads lots of German things and always gets new things from all over the world. He found a small German bookseller there in a narrow alley who collects curiosities and especially pamphlets. He was rummaging around once and said, "I have something for you Herr Starkblom. It must be from you. Well, it was your work 'Vision'. After that, of course, we had the first letter sent to us and the publisher gave us the address and thus found that you were his brother. It's really quite simple and wonderful actually."

The next few hours passed with a restlessness back and forth along with mundane conversation. Starkblom was in an agitated state. Finally, towards evening someone lightly knocked at the door three times. Johannes entered. Marguerite met him quickly blushing and held both hands. The man blinked a little and contented himself with shaking her hands and pressing them to his lips. He wanted to ask her something in a whisper, but she stepped aside and waved at Starkblom. He came closer. "Are you Johannes Starkblom, the son of Adam Starkblom, the shoemaker?"

"I cannot deny it."

"The we are brothers." "Yes, quite certain."

There was a pause. Then the older one began. "We haven't seen each other for a very long time. We don't know each other anymore."

"Well, well," said Johannes briskly. "Let's leave the whole ridiculous situation be. Otherwise things will be terribly uncomfortable. Marguerite must have told you how much we like you – and – well, and so we made an experiment to save you from death. I got the idea because I love life so completely and unspeakably! So how is the situation? I'll sit." When Starkblom was silent, Marguerite said quietly to Hans:

"You were right." The he called out happily, "True? Bravo, bravissimo. So, saved! O, joy! This is the way! Well brother put it there. Now we are brothers!" Karl put his hand in his, but said with an embarrassed smile: "I think Marguerite meant it a little differently about being right. May brotherhood also has another meaning. You — you were supposed to have predicted something in Paris — well, it came true completely in every way." He stood up. "And so there nothing has changed. Isn't that so Marguerite? We two found on another in free love and nothing can separate us – nothing!" Johannes looked at both of them for a long time, then answered "Well, — I was prepared for that. The trip over made me certain. Ah, Marguerite, it would be very distressing for me to live without you! I've become so used to you. Oh, the hell with it, I love you so much! And you — Marguerite? Is everything finished? Well, so be it!"

"No, Johannes, it's not like that: I love you as much as ever. But this love is new. Karl and I – well – you have always denied it, but there is still something to marriage."

Karl had stepped aside and listened quietly. He knew his happiness was secure. Now he took an interest in poor Johannes's fate – that's the thought he held in his mind. "Is there to be a wedding?" Hans asked calmly.

"Well, that depends on how you mean that. So how we lived, wasn't that a marriage?"

"Well the word doesn't matter. It was much better and more beautiful than what is otherwise called an ordinary marriage. It may sound strange, but it's like this: we had what's called a spiritual fellowship."

"Well that's a very bold claim, Marguerite. You must not believe that, brother in spirit. Well, you know what kind of spirit."

Jean, you are irritated, I can hear it in your tone. But I stick by what I said. There couples, at least I've experienced this since I've known Karl, in which the mental and physical are organically connected. Usually it's just a coincidence. It was this way with you and me: their souls are close and their bodies go along with the arrangement out of convenience not out of necessity. The we two belonged together and were good together in every sense isn't the way it was. No, it was never like that!"

"Now I see what you are saying. You have to excuse me, it's been a long story here. The long and short of it is this: there is no place for me! There are only two chairs and they are occupied, yes?" The two were silent.

"I look like a complete fool," Johannes began. "I planned the whole thing. I knew you were my brother when I read the pamphlet. Then a thought crossed my mind. I'll save him through Marguerite! There is only one who could do it. It's been a hell of a ride. I knew you would fall in love with her. It would be a little tragedy, but life would go on. I calculated it to be something like that. And now? Jesus Marguerite, how can it be that you no longer love me and I love you more than ever! Oh, I've missed you these past days! Is there nothing that can be done? Can you change your mind now that I am here? "

"No, Hans," she said. "I really like you and think back on everything and I owe you so much-."

"You don't owe me anything. Oh, you, you!"

"Things are different now. Karl and I belong together. We found each other."

"It's a pity I don't believe in Providence."

"Hm," he mumbled, and smiled despite his being upset.

"Well brother, you are the third person to celebrate. That word doesn't quite fit, but anyway. Well, shall we play a little game of death here? Your mighty eloquence may do something for me now.

"No, Hans," said Karl Starkblom. "I'm not thinking about death for the time being. I hope you will overcome your pain."

"Please, no phrases now. Pain is different. Pain — pain – so this is pain? The word itself doesn't do it justice. Damn it, anyway. I would have called it fear from boredom. I'll have to check again. I have no place to live; I was hoping we could stay here for a while-?" He paused and stood blinking at the two who remained silent. "So, the answer is no? Egoists!"

"Oh, Marguerite!" He suddenly shouted. A passion overcame his artistic poise. The small man trembled all over. Marguerite, you were my companion, laughed with me and endured all my moods patiently. You were so giving, so intimate and understanding. Oh, how dreary I feel now. Uh!"

He sat down. Propping up his head he scratched his beard with his other hand. Suddenly, he looked up.

"I really don't know your situation here in Germany anymore," he began. "Who among your philistines, or professional men or statesmen and the like, who is popular because of their impeccable reputation, humane disposition or in short, their being good men of honor?"

"I don't know at this moment — why are you asking?"

"He'd have to be killed," he said with a smile. They both looked at him in amazement.

"It would have its own charm, no? The world thinks of this and that, but nobody is prepared for *that*. It brings movement to the anthill, and if the perpetrator could just watch it, it would be a curious pleasure."

"You would have no other purpose for doing it?"

"Purpose?"

"Man, how far are you behind in culture? Have you not read your own pamphlets? Or did I misunderstand them? Isn't the purpose not to ask for a purpose? I just have a mind that enjoys such things. Why shouldn't I do it? Maybe I won't. Perhaps when I'm a hundred years old, I'll regret it. It would be a shame then. In any case!"

"This is getting to me," said Starkblom gloomily. "I might have gone with it for a moment, but I can't and certainly not now. I can no longer just say no. I need something to warm to. – Is this the mood of the anarchists? Do you think the same way? "Oh, no," said Marguerite quickly. "Not at all. You want something. Your work has a purpose. Certainly not without nature."

"Still?" Asked Johannes bitterly. "Your old loves. Well, they are not alone, and are as you describe them. Angry and unclear people. I have the defense speech of one you would have 'executed'. In any case you don't know her yet. I'm not an animal. The man's word's shook me to the core. Should I read it to you?"

"Yes," answered Karl briskly. Marguerite called: "Yes, yes!" "I know the man from descriptions, but he was a human being. "Yes, he was," said Hans more solemnly than he was used to. He looked in his breast pocket through all sorts of papers and pulled out a half-tattered newspaper article printed on bad paper. He read: When I take to words, it is not to defend myself against the acts of which I am accused; but only for society which through its faulty organization is responsible for forcing people to continually fight against one another. Don't you see all kinds of people wishing misfortune, not necessarily death) on others for their own advantage? For example, doesn't the businessman wish his competitor would disappear? Doesn't the unemployed wish someone would get fired to open a spot for himself? Well, in such a society one should not be surprised if people do these same things I am accused of.

Since this is the order of the day, when I am hungry, I don't hesitate to use whatever means are at my disposal, even if it means harming someone. Do employers worry that workers will starve when they lay them off? Those who live with abundance, do they care for people who lack basic essential food? Some people give support, but they are powerless to help millions who live in bitter misery and often commit suicide. Yes, societies victims are innumerable. This is how the Hayem family and Mrs. Sonheim acted when they murdered their own children because they couldn't watch them suffer from hunger. All women fear they won't be able to feed their children. They would rather kill the fruit of their love early than see them suffer deprivation and danger.

And all this occurs amidst plenty! It happens in France where everything is in abundance and the butcher's shops are overflowing with meat. Bakeries overflow with bread and garments and shoes are piled high in magazines.

Then others come and say: "All of this is true, but unalterable. Each must come through on his own.

I did this. I didn't want to die of starvation and I didn't calm myself with the thought that after my death a few sympathetic words would be thrown atop my grave. I left that to others. I preferred to become a smuggler, then a counterfeiter, thief and murderer. I could have begged; it is degrading and cowardly and also punished by your laws which make misery a crime! If everyone in need took from those with plenty, perhaps it would quicken the understanding that there is danger in defending the existing social conditions today where uncertainty is permanent and

life is threatened every moment.

One would be far more likely to see that the anarchists are right in saying that in order to maintain moral and physical calm it is necessary to destroy the causes which breed crimes and criminals.

That is why I have done the deeds which I am accused. This is the only logical consequence of the barbaric state of your society. They say one must be cruel to kill his fellow man; but those who speak like that do not see that one only understands what to do so as not to suffer death oneself.

You, the gentlemen of the jury who will in all likelihood sentence me to death, act no different; You judge me because you think it a necessity. You shudder when you hear of murder, but you don't hesitate to kill for a moment when you realize killing is necessary for safety. The only difference between us is that you kill without personal danger, while I risk my freedom and my life.

Gentlemen! You should not condemn the criminals and destroy criminal causes.

There will always be criminals. Today, you will destroy one, tomorrow ten new one will be born. What can be done? Do away with misery which is the seed of crime. And how easy it is to do! It is sufficient to build a society on a new basis, where everything is in common. A place where everyone while producing according to his abilities, consumes according to his needs.

Then you would find neither people like the hermit of Notre Dame, nor those who beg for coin. They are both slave and victim! One would no longer find women who sold their bodies nor would you find men like Pranzini, Prado, Berland, Anastay and others who murder for coins! This all proves very clearly that the cause of all crimes is always the same. One must be mad not to see this.

I am just a simple worker with no education. I have witnessed a life and existence of misery; I feel the injustices of your repressive laws far more than a rich bourgeoisie.

And where do you get the right to kill or imprison a man who, born with the need to live, found himself forced to take what he lacked in order to feed himself?

I have worked to live my own life as long as me and mine have not suffered beyond the measure. I remained what you call 'honest'. Then the work gave out and with the unemployment came the hunger. Only then did the law assert itself, this imperative voice which tolerates no reply; the instinct of self-preservation drove me to commit some of the crimes you accuse me of and which I confess am guilty of committing.

Judge me accordingly, gentlemen of the jury. But if you understand me by condemning me, then judge all the unfortunates whom misery, allied with natural pride, have made criminals and who with a happy livelihood would have remained honest people! I wish that you who are going to sentence me to die, will wear the keepsake of this saying as readily as I place my head under the guillotine blade.

For a while all three were silent. Johannes gnawed his lower lip. Karl looked into space with wide eyes. Marguerite was crying. She was the first to speak up again. She went up to Jahannes and held out her hand. She uttered a single word full of warmth: "Johannes."

He touched her hand and immediately released it. "Well, what good is it to me?" He pointed to Karl. See your – " "What are you looking at Karl? Karl

Starkblom suddenly called out. "I love these people. I can't get away from it."

"From what?"

"From socialism. I believe in it."

"Hm, perhaps, I really don't know myself. It doesn't matter. It'll never come to pass." Karl looked on. Marguerite and Hans left him alone and kept silent.

"Marguerite, quick" said Karl anxiously. "Paper, ink! Quickly. I could forget something. He ran back and forth in the room.

Marguerite fetched the necessary things and Karl quickly wrote a few lines while standing. "I still have something to say," he said. "I have something else on my mind. I want to speak with people again!"

"What are you going to do?" Asked Marguerite. "Another notebook."

"Yes, I just read the note. You may guess what I have in mind."

"Please, Marguerite, read it aloud," asked Johannes.

"Certainly, certainly."

Marguerite hastily deciphered what had been hastily written.

"Utopias, that would be a task I'd be up for writing about. The development of everything that has begun already: psychology, technology, art, town and country, traffic, fellowship, family, nature — in short: everything."

"I like that," said Marguerite. "You can do that."

"You are fortunate," said Johannes, getting up suddenly.

"Perhaps I'll share your happiness later, when Uncle Hans sits by your fire and plays with your children. He'll say with a smile: Children, you owe all this to me. I brought these two together. Well, we aren't so far from each other. Goodbye brother — good luck — I'm serious. I've got to be going now -.

"Goodbye, dear Hans. I definitely wish to see you again. And once you -."

"I'll write when I need money."

"Yes, please write."

"I think this is very likely. Sometimes a line or two, maybe a book. As it goes. Well, I'd better be off -."

"Dear Hans, take care," said Marguerite softly while preparing to bend toward him.

He took a step back and stared at her with his little eyes.

Then he spoke in a trembling voice: "No, Marguerite. We cannot make up for what we have missed at this time. I don't want anyone mow. Pity kisses are no good. I still remember too well -. Well then, goodbye!"

He shook her hand and nodded to Karl. Then he took his hat and walked out the door. He began to sing the Marseilles, then suddenly broke off with a curse. Karl and Marguerite joined hands and looked at each other with an embarrassing smile. Finally, Marguerite said quietly, "Perhaps we should have — no, it wouldn't work. Do you love solitude?"

"I hate it, but I need it. Sitting here reading and writing books and then arguing with the printer over proofs — do you really that was the life I had in mind, in my soul, when I longed to be human again?"

"No, no. I can't get rid of an image I've had as a boy before falling asleep. Me in the middle of a mass of people as a speaker, poet, prophet and leader. Oh, what a mess we've fallen into and we don't know why. Even now, when I write I want to talk and sing and cheer. I turn to people I've never seen scattered throughout the world, here and there. They must hear me, but I've never known them or seen them. Nobody believes that what I see of the people and their institutions and behavior disgusts me. You know, I often have the feeling that I have to bend and squirm with reluctance, turning my innermost being outward. I just want — I don't have the strength. He paused a bit, then took her hand. In a lower voice he said, "You can now see what you mean to me, Marguerite. In all my life you are the first person I've never been disgusted with. Everything we've done has been always natural and beautiful. I believe it will stay that way. Do you know what that means and what you are to me? You're the only one I can live with that feels the same way. Oh, I'm not young enough for loneliness anymore. I want a group of people around me — I've become so modest. I don't want to think of the millions of shining human faces anymore. I renounce the thousands, to find a hundred, perhaps twenty people who I'd surround myself with. Just twenty people I don't feel disgust for; is that asking too much, Marguerite?" She squeezed his hands harder. "Maybe we can find them, Karl. One after another. Johannes?"

"You took the words out of my mouth. I was just thinking about him. I think I understood him and I shall always be able to love him. Maybe he'll come back later. Perhaps. I think it's good he left now, don't you? For now, we need to be alone." He smiled.

"It's been a long day, Karl. Do you wish to rest?"

"You can go rest, Marguerite. First open both windows. I'll stay here a bit and work. When the river rushes below and the night air flows, then a thousand trees sound harmony. I want to dream of it and speak to my people and they will answer me harmoniously with roaring shouts. Nature has opened her senses to be one with us. Thank you, Marguerite. Good night."

Marguerite went out quietly and Starkblom stood by the opened window. He looked out into the darkness for a long while. He watched the tiny lights twinkling in the distance. Lost in a dream he held his hand outside.

Part Six

Utopias by Karl Starkblom Dedicated to my dear wife and our unborn child. I declare solemnly and hope in front of witnesses: I did not shoot myself or otherwise kill myself. I shall not shoot or otherwise kill myself as long as I still feel the vital force in me to work and find joy.

A woman came to me in the early morning in the sunshine. She moved her arm in a wide circle and opened a glittering world to me. She told me there was something wonderfully beautiful about life. In no time I felt the same way. I love life and you Marguerite. She will have my child and we shall abide together. We will certainly not die for a long time.

Do you think I have returned to the pasture of grazing bourgeoisie souls? Do you rejoice at the lost sheep that found its way to the stable late at night and now jumps to its manger with a happy cry?

Indeed, I want to light your sheepfolds and haystacks for you so that sparks fly and blazing fireworks crackle in the sky. Wretched people, how dare you live besides us few who have come to such grief? You crawling along would be considered walking upright. Would that be jubilation of existence little friends? Do you think your toothache (because those are true hard sorrows for you) made life understandable for you? You lukewarm, hapless folk, you know nothing of the coldness the nearness to death can bring nor of the sweltering embers of new life. Away from me! Stay away because I want to look ahead and cheer and laugh.

Nevertheless, I would shoot myself with a painful contorted face and leave this beautiful life. I would tolerate earth. Not one hour more. Yes, even now I suffocate and am torn apart by terrible torment and shame. If I didn't have faith, I would kill myself.

So, I want to ask you and stare into your eyes, all you skeptics and immoral people who travel with me along lonely heights and paths: How can you live? How do you bear it, enjoying yourselves wonderfully? How have you not died by your own hand long since? Reluctantly, I ask you as I put your name in my mouth: I ask you, you Christians, how do you endure your joy and well-being? Some have no faith at all. The rest have no earthly faith — I ask you and implore you: answer me if only in stammer: tell me you know what your comfort rests on, that you know that millions of poor rotting slaves work for you and enable you to lives as you do — how then can you bear up under this fact? You skeptics are no lions. Don't lie. You are neither monsters nor superhumans. You don't believe things can change. Do you honestly believe misery and wretchedness cannot be eradicated? Are you not ashamed that you live? Are you not ashamed of your joys and high life amidst all the mental aches and pains abounding? Can you bear to live?   I ask again and again. And you — again, you Christians wear white silken undergarments which you neither make not clean. You who jingle golden coin in your pockets.

I am not saying these things are undeserved, but merely that others are lacking. You can see the need and misery piled up into the millions. You see the dirt and filth which you yourself do not have to wade through. You see the sweat on others brow which you do not endure and don't help to wipe off. How can you tolerate to live this way? Truly I would be a Christian if I believed in the kingdom of heaven and believed that hardship and sorrow were inevitably arranged by God in the vale of misery — to take my fair share of grief heaped over hardship. I would be a Christian if I wanted to slave, moan and starve and become poorer and poorer to become the most miserable. Ah, but you are Gentlemen? You eat choice meats and cakes and don't choke? The fact that you are clean and others filthy: does that not eat deep into your insides? You have a penny more than the last servant, and it doesn't burn your soul. Yet you live? You enjoy? While others die from want? You breathe easily and deeply in summer freshness while others are tormented with burning lungs look out from filthy cellar windows? This you tolerate? You can bear to live with this? I can't find the right words with mere language! I wrestle and search – oh, villains! You miserable souls! Rascals! You – you rabble!

And with that I spit at you from a distance, you nameless people; for the first time in a long while I haven't, I didn't look past you; now you are dead to me again. Dead. No, I take that word back. Death is too good to give you. The eye can't see you and no ear can hear you. No taste is possible. You are incomprehensible and unintelligible yet there is a stench everywhere; not from the earth or water or air; there is so little collective spark in you all. You are a nameless, inconsequential stench — that is what I find in you people.

I have placed you in very bad company, my beloved skeptics and immoral ones. Haven't you deserved it? Of course, you are disreputable to me. For you live and would do better to die. I say this to you with love and mercy. You are nervous weaklings unable to carry on your shoulders what tyrants and giants from prehistoric times and the wild Renaissance could not. I speak of the lower classes now. You are not blind, but can't see it. You are not deaf, but cannot hear. You hold your beliefs forever and irrevocably – that you should be left in peace. How does that harmonize? This is knocking at your door and cannot be turned away. If as you say, the lower class cannot be lifted, then the upper class would have to be destroyed. You would all go insane, not just a few of you. You would rather die than hear the eternal ever-intensifying knocking, scratching, screaming and roaring — it would drive you all crazy. Do you think this would end? Belief would be childish. He who no longer believes in the Heavenly Father and in eternal life and just retribution, and yet remains so miserable, will not stop rebelling until the earth itself be driven into ruins. And he who does not believe in the hereafter and does not sit in luxury — and soon there will be no more believers — such a one will believe in the earth and in living joyfully and in nascent beauty. It comes again and again knocking and smashing – until a space is carved out where everyone can live in the spirit — because the body and its life force will have become self-evident.

And now, my skeptical friends, I have you where I wanted you. For some time, you have had an objectionable smile on your face. Your voices are being raised! What do you want to attack me with? Aha, I expected that. You'll say I've become a Red cancer again and that the Utopia I just drew in splendid colors has been wiped away again with the sponge of death. This realm of freedom, the graceful lightness of movement, the realm of beauty and drunken flight — this of course is the realm of philosophy. Inside that world, which is of course possible, the smiling question prevails: what does the entirety mean again and again? And there is no answer; forever. This is the mass death of mankind that must now come as a fact of natural necessity. Yes, I have made it known and you got it. And now that you are where I placed you, I ask you once more: Why are you alive? Why don't you die? Do you not believe in the kingdom of beauty and freedom for all born things? Do you not feel the strivings of those servants toward this goal? How dare you live? You have your Marguerite and enjoyments. Slave owners all of you. Those who wish joy and receive none should whip you. Or do you not believe a slave to derive pleasure from beating his master and those that deprive?

I want to tell you what gives me the right to speak to you this way from on high. I am a glittering wave in the river rolling happily towards the sea; You are an unwilling piece of rotting wood being carried away that longs to find a sandy shore to dry and wither in the sun. I not only love myself and my things — woman being the most brilliant of all pleasures — I rush along in the green forest, my companion is not a tender ivy that spoils the strongest oak with its caresses, rather tree after tree we stretch ourselves proudly in the air. Our tops lean in and solemnly whisper while we kiss and talk and dream. I've learned to be human and love humanity again; I stand right in the middle and join in the eternal movement forwards. I believe in the goal, the seriousness and in the beauty. I feel united with the servants and at One with the universe! I am alive! I have the right to live!

Oh, anyone can say that you smile with disgusting familiarity. That's an excuse. I feel like one of those nameless people who promise the kingdom of heaven to the poor in body and spirit. Like one who amuses himself with the world and its earthly enjoyment. Heaven and the future are one and the same. So, a certain Starkblom announced all this earlier. Forsake joy like the poorest souls. If I am honest then I must sacrifice everything for duty's sake. All or nothing – that's what is called for.

Yes, then there is much truth in scorn. It is this too that alone makes us smile bitterly and envelops us in a grey oppressive robe of melancholy. Our life becomes full of contradictions, an inseparable mix that clings to the sweet present and a longing for a glorious future. Since life to me is no more than a walk through the earth and the world of senses, there is no longer any peaceful consequence in our existence. This remains first and foremost in the depths of this experience: I am me and I live and desire my own happiness. We are tangled in the fabric of strivings, in a restless, agonizing, pressing and thrusting time. We have no choice but to hack around in order to gain our place. I am me! I am alive now and never more! I wish to keep my place here.

But I can only live like this if I am passionately ashamed that I have to live like this. I stand on the same ground I am working restlessly to shake and dig up. I only find joy believing that the harvest will soon invite everyone. I can only let others work with me when I have given all my strength for the time when masters and servants no longer exist. O, if you do not understand these contradictions and their necessity, then leave me and this time and this life. It is easy to proscribe with raw force the thousand-colored, multi-toned world of appearance into a formula. It's easy to present a world in a locked state forever. Admittedly it is also easy to surrender the world to annihilation and to preach death to all living things. But now, I preach life for today and all of eternity. As long as I live, I feel united with everything that is alive. As long as I am there, I see and think as a person for the people.

I don't wish to be clear, my friends. But I intuit a lot and see that people have gathered around me and move me along my path. I do not revert to a moral and I never will. As always, I despise many things like you. I am not committed to any formula or party, but remain a human being as long as I live; I want to work in space and time for the growth of the people and the prospering of the earth; I deny many things, but affirm life with a joyful exultation. I have renounced eternal thoughts and thus death. I dream and play. I enjoy my body and soul, my neighbors and most distant ancestors. I feel my strength and passionate instincts and everything else inside of me.

Everything individual threatened to sink into grey nothingness: nature, the dealings of people, technology, the production of needs, science and art. But now everything is interesting to me again.   My eyes are no longer shaded with dull sadness. I open them wide again and look closely at the world. My thoughts our over the earth again.   I dream of immeasurable and unspeakable distances. I want to master everything again and in my own language. I embrace everything that comes near me freely and carefree and confess about everything I know. This is my wish to you leaders of the people: confess what you know!

There is a second thing I ask that may seem strange: you should remain sober! By this I mean you above all, you dreamers and poets and artists and you men of science. Take in your eye with a wide view the whole panorama of culture that opens up with the names: Voltaire, Kant, Goethe, Byron, Schopenhauer.

And then I look at the second picture: steam engines, steam ships and railways, electricity and rational agriculture.

Which changes in spiritual culture correspond to this gigantic change in communication and in the production of the needs of life and enjoyment?

See the second picture as I paint it for you: the brutal spirit of the ascended philistine, spiritless, disgusting lustings for pleasure, barbaric readiness to fight against each other, immense new armies, spiritually and physically, terribly neglected modern slaves, the enormous upsurge in cowardice and hypocrisy, and superstition, the insanity and the isolation of advanced artists and thinkers. Notice the prohibition of free morality, of free thought, free speech — and a free life. Look at this disgusting, sensory-destroying overall picture from a bird's eye view! Which society should it correspond to? And which one will it correspond to?

You should confess, you poets and leaders, you should stretch your hand into the air to curse this common generation. You should swing the scourge over the backs of these Boeotians! [9]

And you should be sober, you dreamers and thinkers, do not continue to burst forth from blue clouds on a romantic steed. You all should see the world as it is, you should be aware of reality and see in it what is possible and what must be. You are to awaken and saddle your will in order to spur it on that you may ride boldly into the land of the future. At least Pegasus is buried with his buckled goose wings, if only the steam horse comes to life for you and the steam plow mixes Europe's soil with fertile seeds. You should sow happiness for the people to come. You must create hope for the ripening seeds are the sower's joy. For the time being, I don't believe in eternal truths. I don't see human reason as being more powerful than a roll of chance. The sun, moon and stars go their laughing way as always without asking about us. Tiny animals and plants build their existence atop innumerable human corpses. And the world begins anew with every child, and chance rules over the change of generations and the course of the stars. For a long time to come, all misgivings will be overturned by unbridled driving passions, and the

---

[9] Relating to Boeotia or its inhabitants. someone dull; obtuse; without cultural refinement.

absurd sum of much smaller independent activities called history. The most difficult struggle of all will go on forever: the struggle between spiritual joy and mental illness. Often, we wish to be sensible but cannot. We wish to flow without thought when we are forced to walk deliberately. But who wants to deny that they are not yet dead, that goddess of reason which begins to grow in reflection of herself? Does the end of the eighteenth-century wake again and again forcing all centuries to walk in its path? Is then the entrance of chance fought at every turn in all areas? And above all when the organization of work is being realized, a milestone only crossed by living free? Does not the fellowship of society become closer to reality along iron rails which turns larger human complexes into one family? Does not science and art entwining lead to the downfall of superstitions that are thousands of years old? There are then revolutions one has forgotten to make; who does not believe that the approaching revolution can completely wash away all the rubbish that is thousands of years old? O, you who believe in gradual development — many enormous things have been going on for some time. The steps you think you still have to climb are long behind us and you didn't notice. What does it matter if you suddenly disappear into oblivion; as long as you are still on top right!

Those of you who take many things for granted, follow me. I repeat the word again that I once uttered. I have always considered socialism possible and took its fulfillment for granted. I feared it because for me life was an abomination. Its arrival would lay bare the innermost core of life. I have nothing against death now either; even now a mood approaches where my soul exults and sings praises. It is comforting and refreshing to know that I can die freely whenever I want. May my mind and tongue wither if I ever slander death!

Let's not hide this from ourselves any longer; our smiling eyes give it away: we all love life immensely! We all make a picture of the world according to our will and we all seek to reshape the earth according to our hearts. We all have a secret lover. Let's fight to capture her! If we all grasp the thought of death in all its majesty, let us drop the petty, wrinkled garb of eternal considerations and immortal philistinism. Words, though so old, wish to be spoken again and again. Since we all live only once and after our death, we are no longer present for the human world and human spirit, let each one of us be great and so free, so cheerful and so careless, so serious and so bold as he is in his own innermost Soul!

Do you know the story of the young man's secret lover? He was timid and did not dare to approach her. And he traveled to foreign countries for many years in order to forget her. But this was not granted to him. Secretly his longing had grown so overwhelmingly, at one point her image rose again in him and would no longer departed from him. This pressed his heart so that it cried out loudly. He returned to his home. But when he saw her again in front of him in her shining beauty, with the high grace of her figure and her movements, which was much more wonderful reality than pale memory had drawn him. Full of shy fear of the fragile beauty, he pressed his soul and made his heart small. When he could no longer stand it, he crept into her bed chamber on a moonless dark night. For a long time, he observed her fine features and looked stunned at the swelling of her breasts. Chaste youth could no longer control itself, and softly, softly, very slowly, so that the sheet did not crackle and she did not wake up, he lay down next to the sleeping girl and he pressed his crossed hands against his chest. His blood thundered and lightning flashed before his eyes. His breath shortened and his skin burned like fire. He could stand the space between him and the beautiful body of the girl. When he could stand no more, he pressed his lips tighter and held his breath. And after he had stopped breathing for a while, his lips opened slowly and his hands fell limply from his chest. His blood was no longer pounding and his flesh was no longer hot. And when secret freedom of the morning awoke, there beside the girl lay dead and cold the timid young man who could have won her.

My compatriots it is not true that freedom in foreign countries is dead and merely a faded word. It is not true. Freedom lives again and again and it is embodied in a special beauty. Let's fight to defy death with joy! Now look at the third picture I paint for you! A feast day. A huge production center where men and women usually spend their mornings stands abandoned today. Today people, in steam cars and electric trams travelled from their villa colonies in small groups to wide meeting places with singing and music. There they are scattered in the art houses and science halls, the playgrounds and dance areas, and still others refresh themselves with wine and food. Later, around noon, the large meeting place fills up, and here public matters are discussed and dealt with, new inventions and scientific statements are communicated, and representatives of opposing opinions often fight each other sharply and resolutely.

In the meantime, the boys and girls have romped around at the games and made new acquaintances across the street with bold shouts and chases. In the afternoon one might like to split up into smaller groups again, drive and go for a walk, row on the river or fly in a balloon into the blue sky. When the sun is about to set, new and old lovers have long since found each other, and here and there in corn rows and hedges they are probably involved in intimate conversation or in a warm embrace. In the evening, when it gets chilly, people probably cover themselves with warm cloths. The darkness brings them closer together again on the wide lawns, from which here and there flares and rockets sometimes fly about. No one thinks about artificially extending the day. One is happy that the darkness envelops its blue wings around the earth. The conversations and the chants now become more solemn and exalted, and now the poets, no longer seen, stand up in the crowd and present for the first time their new works, which they polished in the leisure hours. They sometimes repeat old much-coveted ones and adorn new ones with charming twists. Long into the night you stay together until, when it's warm enough, you fall asleep as you are, or even break up and reach the dwellings.

Of course, it's a dream, otherwise it wouldn't be worth striving for!

It always turns out differently, and perhaps the thoughts that live and grow inside my head are completely different from those that have shaped themselves in the open air. You believe me, don't you, that I still have the strength to be unhappy sometimes? Woe to me if I couldn't experience this anymore!

A strange unholy person visited me recently, my friends, and when I saw him clearly it was part of myself that had grown up in front of me. He was only part of a person and yet in a sense a whole fellow. He told me that his moral sense had long since died out completely, that he had only one principle: if he did not know why a human institution existed, he would try to do the opposite, completely pointless, but only on principle to his own strange delight. He did not know why man should lie and kill; He had no consideration for people and God was not introduced; so, man wants to lie and kill. If you use these words at all then this would be his moral: to draw the endmost consequences to his thinking. Perhaps it couldn't be done, and a kind of shame overcame him although that was too old-fashioned.

Friends, I took you to this hellish place to show you a limit of the conceptions in words and logic. Anyone who has come to this point in their thinking has a decision to make: do they wish to be cold or warm? There is the land of ice-cold language and logic where there is no refutation from the land. Whoever enters it must walk in the footsteps of man, there is no other way. But if you don't want to freeze into this madness, turn away from your thoughts while there is still time.

I am not a moral person, but I ask you: do not be malicious! You have gone too far on a wrong path; if you want to find the right path, you have to go back a little. You are too quick upon your naked sanity. It is not yet time to freeze the soul. Do not do anything whose end you cannot at least foresee. Beware of spiritual malice! Better be an animal at times! That is what I ask of you, you dreamers and thinkers: you should be warm!

And that means to me: You shouldn't be alone, you should join yourselves, you should live your lives alive and leave death to death.

I want to tell you something, my friends, because I can't take it any longer. The giggles and laughter and mudflows have long been rushing in my ears. There are two workers behind my back and they laugh at me. And just now one said to the other: "The stupid guy! What kind of twisted stuff is he talking about? We know stuff thing long ago, almost before we were born, and the other is completely incomprehensible to us, even if he spins it for us a thousand times. We don't have a stomach for such spicy dishes. "

The man is right, absolutely. But, you workers among my comrades, I am not talking to you today. It is true that I place my hope in you above all others; if you weren't there, there would be no transition to what we want. But I'm not talking about that today, I still have a lot on my mind and hope to be able to say it all in time. And "transition" may be the name of the next piece of writing that I am sending you, and in it I am talking about you, the workers!

But today I address completely different people; Today I am speaking to the most dubious and questionable kind of people, to dreamers and thinkers from the bourgeois world. It is not the vanguard of the bourgeoisie, there are only a few who beat their way sideways, this way and that, and they all have something in common. I know them as soon as I meet them, by the bitter expression on their lips and the secret smile in the back of their eyes. So, I call on this youth; they call themselves apostasy and the end of the century, but I still see much that is worth saving in them. I would like to collect them in the field of the future; in the camp of the workers; I would like to enjoin the best of the youth who are weary of culture, that they may surge forward with swiftness and strength.

I am a grown man, but - I say this today with joyful pride - I have achieved what I longed for so ardently, I have become young again. No, I feel I am their lodestar and pathfinder.

At the same time, I am with those young gypsies of the bourgeoisie, whom I encourage to go my way, and at the same time I am with the young workers, to whom I want to bring freedom, not economic freedom that will achieve itself; no, freedom of the individual who looks boldly and carefree towards everything. I do not waver from one side to the other. All opposites are united in me. Life is not contradictory. Only the word is contradictory. My life is young and rich. Follow me all those who can!

Epilogue (1903)

This book was written by a twenty-year old; ten years after it first appeared, I am reissuing it because it has not yet found its readers. Well considered, I think that the two characters in the book, Starkblom and his Marguerite, and also the great Johannes — and perhaps we shall come to know more about him —, who has a small guest role, should become known by all before they sink into oblivion.

Now that I have reread these stormy confessions taken from an excruciatingly happy, capable and, thank God, brave youth, I almost wonder how ironic the external experiences of this Starkblom. The only thing that comes to mind is the scene of the death preacher struggling to button his shirt collar. Friedrich Theodor Vischer[10] and also Gottfried Keller[11] were evidently the godfathers of this book, which was a harbinger of that great revolution that was mistakenly forgotten to be made at the end of the nineteenth century. (The tiredness and interesting pallor that looks so graceful on some of our youth today is probably also due to the great deeds that their fathers failed to do.) So, it is something like inhumane socialism, and anarchism – a turning away from the world, that can be found in this book: A revolution that has turned inward. Outwardly, despite all the agitation reported by him, the man in the book experiences almost nothing; None of his equals live in

---

[10] Friedrich Theodor Vischer (30 June 1807 – 14 September 1887) was a German novelist, poet, playwright, and writer on the philosophy of art. Today, he is mainly remembered as the author of the novel *Auch Einer*, in which he developed the concept of *Die Tücke des Objekts* (the spite of objects), a comic theory that inanimate objects conspire against humans.

[11] Gottfried Keller (19 July 1819 – 15 July 1890) was a Swiss poet and writer of German literature. Keller published the semi-autobiographical novel *Der grüne Heinrich* (Green Henry). It is the most personal of all his works. Under the influence of Jean-Jacques Rousseau's doctrine of a return to nature, this book was at first intended to be a short narrative of the collapse of the life of a young artist.

his Germany; the woman who joins him comes from a romance country. It is the soul with its fantastic, visionary longing that has been created here; and considering the distance that I am from the book today, can I say that many of the pictures of these visions are very beautiful indeed.

Autumn 1903.
Gustav Landauer.